GW00363727

the perfect garden

finishing touches and fabulous effects

the perfect garden

finishing touches and fabulous effects

Creative ideas for transforming your outdoor living space

Tessa Evelegh

Introduction

If you long to relax in a garden with just as much style as your home, but your plant knowledge is elementary and you don't have any enthusiasm for double digging, then it's time to think of your garden in a new way. We're all quite happy to use decoration to give personality to our homes, but traditionally, lovely gardens seem to depend on a grounding in horticulture and lots of hard work. Since a lot of us don't have the time or the knowledge to make a great traditional garden, it's easy to be put off and just make do with a patch of lawn and a few hardy plants. But gardens don't have to be all hard work. There's a lot you can do with very little effort to create great impact in the garden, and then you can sit back and enjoy relaxing outside in your own private plot.

■ ABOVE
A well-thought-out garden will bring you many, many happy hours.

■ OPPOSITE
A half-concealed entrance to a secret place adds a delightful air of mystery.

Introduction

The key is to take your interior decorating ideas and skills and to adapt them for the outside of your home. A splash of paint outside can have just the same impact as it does inside. "Flooring" outside doesn't have to be limited to the ubiquitous green carpet of grass. There are plenty of other choices: flagstones, pavers, cobbles, wooden decking or brick. You can add fixtures and fittings, furniture and decorative touches such as pictures, sculpture, ornaments, lighting and painted pots, in just the same way as you would indoors.

This is just a taste of the many ideas packed into the pages of this book, which, I hope, will inspire you to think of your garden in a new way so that you can really make the most of your outdoor space, even if your plant knowledge is all but non-existent.

And don't be put off if you think your garden is either too small to bother with, or so large that gardening has become an elephantine task. The smallest garden can become the most successful decorated garden room for all the family if it is well-planned to include eating and play areas. If your garden is large, you could just decorate the patio area for entertaining to begin with and

■ ABOVE
Pots of leafy evergreens always look charming on a flight of old steps.

■ BELOW
Carefully trained trees form a cool and shady canopy for hot summer days.

■ ABOVE
Colourful plants spill over exuberantly on to a path of brick, their sharp pinks and purples enhancing its roseate tones.

work round to other areas when you have the time and the funds. Large or small, the best way to get the most from any garden is to set up a comfortable seating and/or eating area, so it's always ready for relaxing and entertaining. No need to wait for high summer before you sit outside: if everything is at hand, it's easy to carry out food or drinks, even on fine spring days.

STARTING FROM SCRATCH

There are lots of ideas in the pages of this book that can be introduced into an established garden. It's when you have a "blank canvas" that the whole operation becomes somewhat daunting.

Although the idea of decorating the garden in the same way as you would a house, taking away the need for a wealth of horticultural knowledge, makes the whole project a little more attainable, there are extra dimensions to gardens that need to be addressed.

The most obvious one is that every garden has some planting, and even the most hardy slow-growing plants will grow, altering the structure of the garden as they go. The other big difference between indoors and outdoors is the levels. Inside, floors are flat. Outside, the ground may not be, and, if it is, you may want to alter the levels to add interest. A step up or a step down can completely change the space.

You may also want to divide the garden into different areas, which also adds interest. You can do this with levels, or with low walls or trellis screens. If you want to add such elements to the garden, and you don't feel confident about planning hard landscape yourself, you may want to bring in the help of a garden designer. Whatever your decision, the key is not to be fazed by this basic planning.

Start by making a list of your needs and wants. Where would you like the patio area? It is usually situated right next to the house, but it doesn't have to be if there's another part of the garden that gets more sun. Do you want a water feature? Do you need a play area? Is there room for ball games, or is your backyard too small? Would a sandpit, play house or climbing frame, which all use up less space, be more suitable? How much planting area do you want? Is space more important to you, or do you find tending plants relaxing? Do you want a lawn, or, especially if space is limited, would it be better to pave the area? Where will you store lawnmowers, tools, pots and compost (soil mix)?

Such a list will help you to work out the areas you need, whether you decide to plan out the space yourself or you get someone else to do it for you. The ground planning is key because once the levels, patio and planting areas are sorted, the garden has a structure you can build on.

FIXTURES AND FITTINGS

Permanent structures lend personality to a home. They're not part of the architecture, so they reflect the style of the current owner, yet they have an air of permanence that furnishings and accessories could never give. Fixtures and fittings are the easiest way to impress your personality on the garden. Fit a small garden building, an arbour, an arch or pergola, some trellis or simply some shelves for general storage or displays of potted plants, and you'll see an immediate change. These may seem like big projects, but with garden buildings in kit form and a variety of trellis panels available from most garden centres, there's a lot you can do in a weekend. Once built, structures can be customized with MDF (medium-density fiberboard), fretwork and paints or stains for an easy-to-build but highly individual finished effect.

THE BASIC DECORATING

The quickest way to introduce all-year colour into the garden is to paint it on. No worrying about what will flower when, or how to keep the colour going through the winter – it's there for keeps. Adding colour in the garden with paint and stain has become easier in recent years as there's a much wider choice of exterior paints and stains. Where once we were limited to pine green or various shades of brown, now turquoise greens, pinks, blues and lilacs are being added to the repertoire available to the general public. Use it to paint fences, trellis work and garden buildings, then, to add to the impact, you can plan the planting to complement the colour scheme. Quite apart from the finished effect, one advantage of painting the fences is that even while the plants are immature the garden doesn't look quite so naked.

SOFT FURNISHINGS

Once the basic decorating is done, you can begin to choose the soft furnishings, which, in the garden, is the planting. If you're a novice, and you don't want to spend hours nurturing plants, the best solution is to choose traditional favourite evergreens, shrubs, climbers and perennials. These have become popular because they almost always grow successfully. Evergreens and trees are all hardy provided they are given plenty of water during their first year. They can be used to provide structure to the planting, and can be supplemented by easy-to-grow shrubs that show plenty of colour, such as fuchsia, hebe, pyracantha, hydrangea, weigela and shrub roses. Hardy climbers that can be used to furnish fences include climbing roses, honeysuckle, clematis and jasmine. Easy-to-grow herbaceous plants that die down in winter but return year after year include *Alchemilla mollis*, *euphorbia* and border *Geranium* (Cranesbill). If in doubt, buy plants that are in plentiful supply in the garden centre since these are usually the popular easy-to-grow varieties. Check the flowering or berrying period to make sure they weren't put on show in the only week they bloom, and check the height and spread they will reach

■ LEFT
Loose hedging, tied in an arch over a pathway and studded with flowers, divides a garden into areas of interest.

■ LEFT
Setting out one or two seats in a sunny corner of the garden and adding potfuls of plant colour will give you an instant and irresistible al fresco room.

when mature. All this information should be on the plant label.

For instant colour, which you can use to supplement the planting, pot seasonal bedding plants into containers. These can be used to decorate the patio, as a focal point in the garden, or even placed in the borders to boost the colour between seasons.

Buy young plants from the garden centre that are already showing colour and plant them in pots, adding fertilizer to be sure of a splashy show. Keep them moist and deadhead them regularly for a long flowering season. The advantage of containers is that once they have finished flowering they can be moved to a more secluded part of the garden, while others, coming into bloom, can be moved to centre stage.

DECORATIVE FEATURES

Inside, you probably have paintings, lighting, ornaments and sculpture, vases of flowers and potted plants, which all add decorative personality to the home. With a little thought, it's easy to see how you can decorate the garden with the outdoor equivalents.

Mosaics make perfect all-weather outdoor art, and can be used as pictures, sculptures or even to decorate furniture. Scarecrows can be outdoor sculpture, as can piles of pots, groups of watering cans and old tools or the more obvious fountains and wall masks. Bird-feeding tables, bird baths and birdhouses become ornaments, as do painted pots and wind chimes. Stamp your style on your garden using all of these, perhaps keeping to a colour theme for continuity.

FURNISHING THE GARDEN

Although the garden furniture is really the finishing touch to the garden, it can also be the very first thing you do. Even if you don't have the time or the budget to make over the garden, if you do nothing else, it's worth making a comfortable seating area so that everything is in place for relaxing in the garden – be it reading a book on your own or inviting friends over for a meal. If you're planning the garden from scratch, you may like to think about built-in furniture – a bench under a pergola, for example. If not, invest in all-weather furniture that doesn't have to be dragged in and out every day. It doesn't have to be expensive, though it does need to be comfortable. Add cushions and throws to any that falls short of the mark.

You can give the seating area a relaxing ambience by aiming to stimulate all the senses. Glean visual inspiration from the pages of this book and add perfume by choosing scented varieties of plant, such as honeysuckle, old-fashioned roses, summer jasmine and tobacco plants. Smell stimulates the tastebuds, too, so add in some sweet-smelling herbs such as marjoram, sage or rosemary and potted summer fruits, such as strawberries. Bring on the music with wind chimes or a water feature, and add soft feathery foliage such as love-in-a-mist for that touchy-feely element.

IN A NUTSHELL

Think of your garden as a place to relax: plan it to suit you and your lifestyle; decorate it as boldly as you would your home using paint, stain, flowers and foliage for your favourite colour palette; furnish it for comfort; add finishing touches, scents and sound for ambience; then sit back and enjoy.

PLANNING A GARDEN FOR LIVING IN

The first step to decorating your garden is the planning. Take time to think about what you want from your space, and remember that the smallest plot merits as much thought as the most sprawling of areas.

Decide what is important to you, whether it is an array of brightly-coloured flowers, a shady arbour for quiet contemplation, or a fun play area for energetic children. Whatever you want from your garden, there are three main elements to consider: privacy, atmosphere and the plantings. Setting the right mood in your garden can be easily achieved through the placing of an ornament here or a scented plant there: this book will give you ideas for a garden retreat that has year-round appeal in colour, texture and fragrance.

■ ABOVE
A garden can be many things, but ultimately it is a place for relaxation.

■ OPPOSITE
The finer points of an ornamental bird bath may be lost on birds, but they will still return to your garden again and again for drinking water and bathing.

Inspirational Ideas

The most relaxing and visually pleasing gardens are usually the result of careful planning. You will need to consider how best to use the available space, the vistas you can create and the ambience of the garden, to prepare the "canvas" for your decorative touches. Once you begin to reap the rewards of such forethought, you will certainly feel it was all worthwhile.

■ OPPOSITE
Delicate ornamentation can be inappropriate for utilitarian areas of the garden, such as vegetable patches, which need to withstand heavy-duty usage. However, these plots will blend nicely with the garden if well laid out and decorated simply with splashes of colour.

A good place to start is to consider what you want from your garden. You will probably want somewhere to sit and, perhaps, eat. If you have children, you will want space for them to play, and you will also need to provide some kind of storage area for tools, pots and other garden paraphernalia. All this is perfectly possible, even in a tiny garden. An area 2m/6½ft square is sufficient space in which to sit and eat. Children would be thrilled with a sandpit, even one of just 90cm/3ft square and, if there is just a little more space, there will be room for a small play house.

Plan out in your mind the best place for each of these activities in much the same way as you might plan your kitchen, where you also need to allocate space for working, eating and leisure. Once these priorities are fixed, it will be much easier to work out the layout of the garden. This is important, even if you won't have the resources for new paving and landscaping in the foreseeable future. For example, there may be a flower bed just where you feel it would be best to create a seating area. With the garden layout left as it is, you will continually have to bring furniture in and out when you need it. That is tiresome and no more convenient than a sitting room would be if you had to bring in a chair every time you wanted to relax. However, with a few little changes, such as turfing over a surplus flower bed, you can organize the garden so it is ready for relaxation any time you want.

Once the main areas are worked out, it is much easier to decide where you want to have planting areas, and within this framework you will be able to transform the space into a decorative outdoor room that you will want to use for much more of the year than just the few months of summer.

■ LEFT
Dividing up the space in your garden creates visual depth. Here, box orbs help to define a vista of the arbour at the end.

■ ABOVE
Garden paraphernalia displayed on a wire shelf transforms the functional into the decorative.

■ BELOW
Low hedging is cleverly used here for a rich and interesting design, to form visual divides and create several rooms within one garden.

Planning for Privacy

You will only be able to relax in the garden once you have organized the basic needs: privacy and shelter. Without the benefit of enclosed spaces, especially in built-up areas, these considerations can be problematic. However, there are ways of achieving them. Trellises can be fixed on top of walls and fences to create extra height: cover them with decorative climbers. You could plant fast-growing conifers, such as thuja, but check their potential height when mature or you could end up not so much overlooked as overshadowed.

Privacy is particular important for seating areas. Even if you live in the middle of the country and have a huge garden, you will feel much more comfortable if you site seating where, at least on one side, there is the protection of a screen of some sort. This could be the garden boundary wall, a hedge or even trellis arranged to lend a more intimate feel.

PRIVACY FROM ABOVE

If you are closely overlooked, you may also want to create privacy from above. One of the most successful ways of doing this is to create a pergola and encourage it to become entwined with vines or other climbers. That way, you have a "roof", which filters the natural light and allows a free flow of fresh air underneath.

PLANTS FOR SCREENING

Buxus sempervirens
Carpinus betulus
Chamaecyparis lawsoniana 'Green Hedger'
Crataegus monogyna
Elaeagnus ebbingei
Escallonia 'Iveyi'
Fagus sylvatica
Fargesia nitida
Griselinia littoralis
Ilex aquifolium
Ligustrum ovalifolium
Osmanthus delavayi
Prunus cerasifera
Prunus laurocerasus
Pyracantha 'Mohave'
Taxus baccata
Thuja orientalis
Ulmus parvifolia
Viburnum rhytidophyllum

■ RIGHT
Let the scent of verbena and honeysuckle perfume this outdoor room. Edwardian ironwork lends an air of bygone elegance to this brick bay.

■ LEFT
The sense of privacy offered by an enclosed space lends a romantic touch to any garden. Here, a combination of trees, shrubs and potted plants has created an intimate patio area at one side of the garden lawn.

■ OPPOSITE
A combination of trees and plants of different heights is used in this flower-bed to screen one part of the garden from the next.

■ LEFT
Secret places can be created in even the smallest of spaces. This pathway winds through plantings in a tiny 3m/10ft plot.

■ BELOW
Even in a large garden that is not overlooked, a seating area is more comfortable if it is sheltered and secluded. Here, two rustic wattle hurdles have been used to create an informal outdoor "room".

Atmosphere and Romance

Once space in the garden has been defined, you can begin to set the mood. Creating ambience relies on stimulating the senses, and sight, sound, touch, taste and smell are all supplied free of charge by nature. Simply by being outside, you are closer to nature, so it should be easier to bring atmosphere and romance into your garden than anywhere else in your home. Finding ways to stimulate each of the senses is what this book is all about, and these pages are packed with decorative ideas to enhance the garden.

A SENSUOUS GARDEN

Combined with the visual delights offered by the plants, a garden planned for the senses will produce inspired results. In addition to the sound of birdsong and the buzzing of insects, you can add the music of wind chimes or the evocative trickling of water in even the smallest plot. The garden also provides the most glorious fragrances, both sweet – from flowers such as roses, honeysuckle and jasmine – and aromatic – from lavender and piquant herbs. Touch, too, can be stimulated as it is impossible to walk through a garden without being touched by – or reaching out to touch – some of the plants; this is especially pleasing if they have interesting textures: try to include a range of fleshy, frondy and feathery plants. Finally, eating out in the garden contributes taste to complete the sensory picture.

OUTDOOR INTIMACY

The most romantic gardens always give a hint of intimacy. They could literally be enclosed outdoor rooms, such as courtyards, balconies or roof gardens, which automatically offer a private area. If your space is larger, you can add romantic interest by building separations in to the garden to create hidden places. This isn't as difficult as it sounds, and can be made a highly successful feature of even the smallest gardens. You can put a door in a fence or wall to hint at another space; add dividers to give the feeling of moving from one area to another, or provide screening for an eating area.

These dividing tactics also create the illusion of space. Adding a separation means you are able to see beyond one area into another, which lends perspective to the whole space, giving it structure and shape. However light the screening, it hints at secret places and romance.

■ LEFT
Springtime blossom flutters to the ground through this delicate ogee archway, which gives the feeling that one is moving out of one area of the garden into another.

■ ABOVE
Colourful mosaic tiles add tactile interest and visual appeal to a shady area of the garden.

■ ABOVE
Dining al fresco means seasonal food and delightfully simple table decorations.

■ ABOVE
Seedheads and Chinese lanterns hung up to dry supply bright colour.

■ LEFT
It is impossible to wander down this path without reaching out to touch the exuberant bushes of scented lavender.

■ RIGHT
A very modern mosaic, in the style of a Mexican ceramic sun, set against a brick wall, adds immeasurably to the atmosphere of the garden.

■ BELOW
Water flows elegantly over this exquisite, wall-mounted, cast-iron lily pad. The sound of trickling water enhances any outdoor area, and a water feature such as this, attached to a wall, need not take up an inordinate amount of space.

■ RIGHT
A miniature courtyard is set out as an enchanting outdoor room. The cherry tree suggests pretty "wallpaper", while the fallen blossom forms a natural carpet. There is even a "coffee table" positioned in front of the bench, and an alcove is set in the wall.

Finding the Levels

Whereas indoors you would prefer your floor to be level, outside the opposite is true. This is probably because inside the various heights of furniture automatically give you interesting levels and furniture tends to occupy a greater proportion of the floor space. Outside, even a furnished garden has greater expanses of floor space, which could result in monotony. Unless you are considering a very tiny garden space, similar in size to a room indoors, or you have decided to have a particularly formal design, such as a knot garden or parterre, you will probably want to create some change in level.

Adding a split-level dimension to your garden can be as simple as raising one area above another by the height of just one single step. If you are not in a position to re-landscape your garden for the sake of a change of level, there is still a lot you can do. Add staging at one side and use it to display potted plants; use a plant stand to lend height; make a feature of garden buildings to give architectural interest; or use plants of various heights to create changes of level.

■ OPPOSITE
A pretty Victorian wire plant stand, filled with flowering plants, brings flashes of white high up in the middle of a largely green planting area.

■ ABOVE
Flowering climbers, such as clematis, don't have to be restricted to walls and fences. By training them up obelisks, you can take the colour even higher.

■ LEFT
Even in a tiny patio area, there is room to create levels. Here, raised beds are built in white-painted brick to match the garden floor.

Planning the Planting

Herbaceous borders provide wonderful colour in summer but die down to next to nothing in winter, so it is good to provide an evergreen structure of plants to see you through the seasons. These will contribute to the "architecture" of the garden, creating levels, screens and sculpture, and a backdrop of deep colour to offset the plants and flowers.

The arrangement of shrubs in the garden can introduce all manner of interesting design features. Plan to have taller shrubs at the back of the borders, slowly graduating towards the front, or you can make more structured steps. You can arrange rows of small, lightly screening plants across the garden to create a living screen, and you can use specimen trees or trimmed topiary as living sculpture.

The colour scheme for the rest of the planting can be planned around this basic structure, but the structural shrubs and trees can also be chosen to ensure some colour all year round: include fruit trees for blossom in early spring, shrub roses for summer colour, late-flowering clematis and wonderful berries, such as those of pyracantha in autumn and holly in winter. This display of year-round colour can be added to and complemented with a collection of carefully-chosen autumn-flowering bulbs such as colchicum, schizostylus and cyclamen.

CONTAINER CHOICES

The most flexible colour is added with pots and containers. By planting up moveable pots you can put the colour where you want it, and re-plant with new seasonal colour as the old blooms die down. Pot up bulbs in the autumn in anticipation of spring colour and, as they die down, put them in a secluded part of the garden for their leaves to soak up the light, ensuring a better show next year.

Colour creates far more impact if you keep it to a theme – blues and pinks, perhaps, or oranges and yellows – and this theme can be strengthened with the use of paint and wood stain on nearby fences, garden buildings, furniture or on the pots themselves.

With the introduction of comfortable furniture, and with the finishing touches of accessories and decorations, a garden quickly becomes an outdoor room ready for entertaining and relaxation.

■ ABOVE
A beautiful specimen plant, such as this standard rose, makes a delightful feature in an unusual container.

■ ABOVE RIGHT
A well-established honeysuckle will form a living scented screen in the garden, gathering to it all forms of butterflies and bees.

■ RIGHT
Seasonal flowers look lovely potted up and grouped for massed colour. Containers allow you to move the colour around the garden to create focal points wherever you want them.

■ LEFT
You can use garden flowers outside in the same way as you might use potted plants inside. Here, spring flowers make a charming window sill display.

■ LEFT
Erect an evergreen archway to create an illusion of space. The glimpse of another area leads perspective to the whole garden, adding structure and depth.

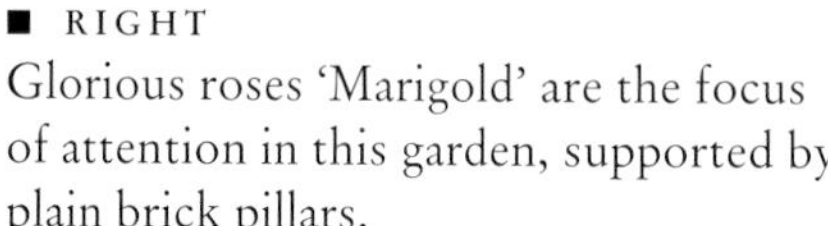

■ RIGHT
Glorious roses 'Marigold' are the focus of attention in this garden, supported by plain brick pillars.

■ ABOVE
After the springtime glory of its blossom, this small apple tree once more takes the centre stage in the garden as the beautiful white clematis 'Marie Boisselot' grows up through the branches.

Decorative Garden Floors and Walls

The floor and walls offer the basic structure to the garden room, setting the tone in stone or brick, wood, gravel or grass. And even though these elements may seem fixed, there is still scope for decoration with imagination and flair.

For visual impact, you can combine hard and soft textures, setting a Victorian rope-effect edging next to an emerald lawn, for example, or you can vary the levels. A floor patterned with tiles can have an instant decorative effect, while planting a lawn with chamomile in place of grass will provide a beautifully subtle fragrance when walked on.

Gardens walls can provide interest at different levels. Don't be afraid of using indoor effects such as shelving or pictures for an eye-level display.

■ ABOVE
Old stone steps provide the backdrop for a wealth of summer colour.

■ OPPOSITE
Vertical lines on this path draw the eye to a distant vista and a welcome garden seat.

FLOORS: THE PLACE TO START

Outside, even more than in, the "floor" has a huge impact on the overall effect, and decorating your garden has to start with the groundwork. Perversely, the smaller the area, the harder the floor has to work. Where there is plenty of space, sweeping lawns are fine. Where space is at a premium, it may hardly seem worth getting the mower out, and a combination of hard and soft surfaces becomes more sensible and visually pleasing.

Just as inside the house, the basic choice outside comes down to one between hard and soft flooring – the hard being patios and paths, the soft being planting. But while a single floor surface running seamlessly from wall to wall looks wonderful inside, outside, in anything but the smallest patio, it is likely to look flat and dull. Introduce variation, texture and a change of levels to create a much more interesting vista.

If you can afford it, and you want to start from scratch, it really is worth getting the floor right, as that offers the best basic structure to the garden. Even the most charming planting, pots and decorative details are diminished when set against the tedium of uniform concrete slabs, while a well-thought-out floor looks elegant even before you add a single plant. And in later years, it will be much easier to make a complete change in the planting, the pots, even the boundaries, in order to create a new look, rather than structuring the ground.

Even if it really isn't feasible to make a major change, there are ways to improve the situation – perhaps by removing some of the paving slabs to increase planting space, both around the perimeters and within the main paved areas. Or you could use decorative detailing to disguise parts of a less-than-pretty surface.

■ BELOW
A small paved patio teeming with plants and pots of different heights.

■ LEFT
The clay-tiled floor and brick retaining walls of an old, demolished greenhouse make an evocative setting for a herb garden and a focal point within the whole context of this established garden. A similar effect could be achieved using new tiles designed for outside use, laid diagonally in alternating colours.

■ LEFT
A soft green lawn creates a smooth carpet along the length of this shady walkway.

■ BELOW
A raised bed of brick set on gravel provides easy access for the gardener, and the geometric design mimics the formality of classical gardens.

■ RIGHT
This tapestry of purple and lilac planting, bordering a herringbone-patterned brick path, is reminiscent of a soft carpet laid on parquet flooring. Mosses, alpines and other low-growing plants have been allowed to take up residence on the curved English York stone steps.

Surface Choices

Flooring occupies the greatest area of the garden, and as such it will have a huge impact on both the visual aspect of your outdoor space and the practicalities required for its upkeep. The choice of flooring will depend partly on budget and the availability of materials in your locality, and partly on the look you set out to achieve. The most successful choice of surfacing will finally be a compromise between function and appearance.

■ OPPOSITE
A sweeping lawn makes an enviable natural emerald carpet, perfect for wetter climates. An expanse of cool, green grass punctuates the visually busy areas of planting, inducing a sense of calm in the garden.

Choosing your hard surface material can be difficult. Outdoors, little surpasses the beauty of natural stone, especially a local stone, which will harmonize with its surroundings. Another good material to use is frostproof flat-surfaced brick; specially made brick pavers are the ideal choice for patios and paths. Aggregates, in the form or gravel or shingle, are another form of natural stone. Other decorative hard surfaces can be achieved with a clever use of pebbles, slate or ceramics.

If such materials exceed your budget, there is a wide choice of concrete pavers. Not all are uniform, uninspired slabs: many have subtle variations of tone to give a naturally aged look; some come in the form of ready-to-split blocks of cobbles, each of which comes away slightly differently for a more natural effect.

Not-so-hard underfoot floorings can be made of wood: this may be custom-made timber decking or reclaimed materials such as railway sleepers (ties). When it comes to soft flooring, the obvious solution is a lawn; bear it in mind that herbs such as chamomile or thyme can make interesting alternatives to grass. Planting also offers a soft floor, though this will only be suitable for a look-but-don't-walk area.

The choice of material is one thing, deciding on its best form for your garden is another. Stone is available in rectangular slabs, squares, cobbles or crazy paving; concrete comes in any number of shapes. The form you choose and the way in which the material is laid can affect the whole look of the garden. Smaller units can make a tiny plot seem larger. Bricks laid widthways across a path give a tranquil look; laid lengthways they lend dynamism. A herringbone arrangement looks both attractive and established. Using differently sized units of the same material offers variety, while laying materials diagonally can visually enlarge a tiny area.

The surface you choose should always fulfil its function. Wooden decking laid under overhanging trees will quickly become covered with slippery algae. If children are going to play daily on a patio, you may find that flat slabs are more useful than characterful old bricks.

■ LEFT
Small pavers laid end-to-end visually elongate the curved path in this small garden, leading the eye through the planting, which is contained by the well-defined path edge.

STEPPING UP

Changing the level in a garden immediately adds an extra dimension. Even a single step gives the feeling of moving from one area to another, while lending visual depth to the whole garden. Flights of more than two steps need plenty of space and can quickly eat into a small garden, as each one needs to be at least 30cm/12in deep, and shallow enough to make them easy and safe to negotiate, especially in wet or frosty weather.

Flights of stairs leading down to the garden can be a real bonus, because it doesn't take much effort to make a feature of them. Pots of plants on each step always look charming, especially if they end in a flourish at the bottom with a carefully arranged group.

■ ABOVE
Steps leading from the courtyard are framed with a mass of exuberantly flowering plants, which soften the harsh line of the stair rail.

■ ABOVE
Miniature violas, one plant to a pot, make an enchanting decoration for weathered old stone steps.

■ LEFT
A few small steps leading to a doorway form the perfect stage for a cluster of containers. This group of evergreens is augmented for the festive season by a potted topiary tree of blue spruce and fir cones.

■ RIGHT
Changes of texture as well as levels give definition to garden spaces. Here, a feature has been made of little-used weathered wooden steps, which rise from a cobblestone courtyard.

■ BELOW
Risers of plain stone steps make the perfect setting for a charming decorative detail, like this line of mosaic flowers.

FLOOR EDGINGS

The way a path or patio is edged plays an important part in the design of the flooring. Many well-designed pavers and setts (small cobble-like pavers) have complementary kerb edging.

One idea is to make edgings by laying pavers in a different direction to the rest of the path or patio, or setting them on their sides to create a ridge. Bricks can be set at an angle to make a zigzag edge. Specially designed edges in stone, brick, concrete and metal are also available. Alternatively, you can create your own border in, say, shells or corks "planted" upright at the edge of a flower bed. You could also grow a neat miniature hedge of box or lavender, but this would need trimming or pruning from time to time.

■ ABOVE
Original Victorian rope edgings are enjoying renewed popularity, and are particularly suited to the gardens of older houses and cottages. Many new variations of rope edging are now available for a more contemporary look.

■ ABOVE
These antique, charcoal-coloured clay edging tiles aligned in a row would provide a neat finish to a pathway or terrace in a formal town garden.

■ LEFT
Scallop shells left over from the dinner table or cajoled from the fishmonger make a delightful edging in shades of soft coral that co-ordinate well with terracotta paving. Because edging materials do not need to be particularly durable, they offer an almost limitless number of decorative possibilities.

Making Patterns

There is a great tradition of elaborate "floors" for outside use. The Romans created intricate mosaics on courtyard floors, a skill that reached its zenith in richly decorated Islamic outdoor pavements. In the Middle East and India, decorative walkways were composed of ceramic tiles laid in geometric patterns.

Echoes of highly intricate and decorative floor styles can be seen in Victorian English architecture: many terraced houses are approached by "tessellated" pathways, with square, rectangular and triangular tiles laid in formal patterns of contrasting colours – black and white, or cream, chocolate and terracotta.

Pebbles are another traditional mosaic material, and their natural colours and smoothly rounded forms can be used to make exquisite textural panels or complete garden floors. Simple geometric shapes are traditional, though in the hands of an artist they can become elaborate, figurative works of art.

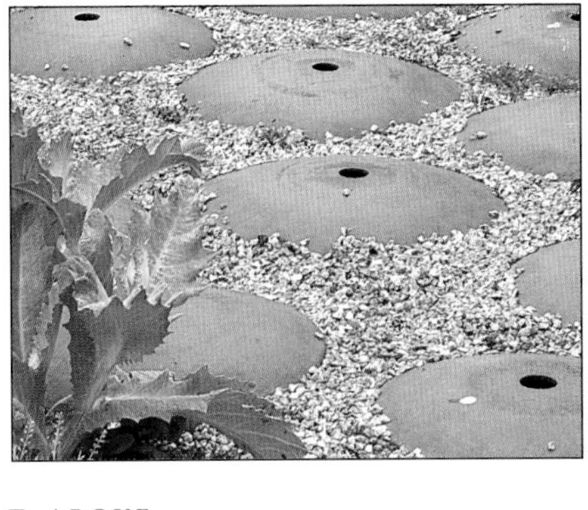

■ ABOVE
Even old hub caps from agricultural machinery can be used to add texture to an ordinary gravel pathway.

■ ABOVE
Pieces of water-worn slate collected from the beach and set edge on in mortar make an elegant textural plaque. In spring, forget-me-nots can be planted round it to create a vibrant azure border.

■ ABOVE
Tessellated tiles, rescued from a crumbling city pathway and destined for a builder's skip, make an enchanting detail in a flower bed.

■ ABOVE
Even artefacts as unprepossessing as old drain covers look good when grouped together, creating a pleasing effect with their simple geometry.

Floor Plantings

Outdoor flooring looks more established if small mosses, plants and lichens are allowed to grow between the pavers – though the effect can be enhanced by a little judicious weeding: self-seeded violas look enchanting, but thistles are less appealing.

Floor patterns using plants rather than hard materials have been created throughout the ages. The most obvious examples of these are Elizabethan knot gardens and baroque parterres. In these, an outline shape is formed using hedging in straight lines, geometric patterns or curves to create, in the case of a knot garden, an elaborate knot effect. Traditionally, different plants are then grown within each section of the knot. Parterres can be on a much grander scale, and often incorporate topiary, lawns and highly formalized plantings. At a more affordable level, you can cultivate mini-gardens or "lawns" by removing a paver and introducing low-growing plants in its place. This is a particularly effective way of softening uninspiring areas of large concrete slabs. Try planting a miniature herb lawn that releases its aroma as you brush past. Chamomile (the non-flowering variety 'Treneague') and thyme are particularly effective. Or you can plant larger herbs, such as lavender and sage. Low-growing flowers, such as alyssum, violets, violas, pinks or any of the alpines, will provide a subtle but telling splash of floor-level colour.

■ ABOVE
A carpet of leafy green foliage sprouting up between the cracks in the concrete gives this garden corner an appealing summer look.

■ ABOVE
An alpine garden planted into an old millstone gives this floor an extra dimension.

■ ABOVE
This fascinating three-dimensional, ceramic sun makes an original floor feature. Planted with low-growing plants, such as "mind-your-own-business" (*Soleirolia soleirolii*), it takes on the appearance of a rich green tapestry that enhances the sun motif.

Alpine Wheel

There is something very appealing about alpines. The wonderfully varied texture of their foliage is punctuated in the spring with the most delicate-looking flowers. They are not difficult to look after, and will eventually spread to create a rich tapestry. This wheel makes a more original home for alpines than the typical rock garden, and would be more appropriate for a formal garden. Make the wheel as small or as large as you like, and calculate the number of plants you will need by checking the extent of their eventual spread.

Tools and Materials

For a wheel about 2.4m/8ft in diameter:

- 2 wooden pegs
- string
- spade
- garden compost (soil mix) or rotted manure
- fertilizer
- heavy, metal circular cover
- 64 bricks
- about 3 alpine plants with a 30cm/1ft spread per section
- gravel
- large pebbles and slates for decoration

■ LEFT
Use decorative beach pebbles and pieces of slate to add textural interest to the newly planted wheel. The alpines will gradually spread over the gravel, virtually filling the sections.

1 Make a pair of compasses by tying a wooden peg to each end of a piece of string the length of the radius of the wheel. Dig over the approximate area of the wheel and prepare the soil by adding compost (soil mix) or manure and fertilizer. Use the compasses to mark out the circle and place the circular cover in the centre. Position bricks around the circle and across the centre to form the "spokes".

2 Arrange the alpine plants between the spokes of the wheel. Here, each section has been planted with a different variety of alpines, so that as they grow they will help to define the design.

3 Carefully sprinkle a layer of gravel between and around the plants to keep the soil in place. Finally, complete the design with large pebbles and slates, dotted attractively between the plants.

Pretty Pebble Rug

Create an outdoor "fireside rug" from pebbles, broken garden pots and old china ginger-jar tops. Choose a simple design that is not difficult to achieve: you can always add to it as your confidence grows. The "rug" will make an appealing, witty motif in any paved patio or terrace.

■ RIGHT
The subtle colour variations of natural stones, slate and terracotta harmonize beautifully in this decorative panel.

PREPARATION

The bed on which the "rug" is to be set should be prepared to a depth of about 10cm/4in, allowing a 5cm/2in clearance below the level of the rest of the paving. Dig out the area to the dimensions of the panel and to a depth of 15cm/6in. Mix equal parts of fine aggregate and cement. Then, using a watering can, dribble in water a little at a time until you have a dry, crumbly mix. Use this mix to fill the area, leaving a 5cm/2in clearance. Level and allow the mix to dry. Gather together plenty of materials for the design and lay them out for size on the dry bed before you begin. Using tile nippers, cut off the bottoms of at least six terracotta pots and snip off the rims in sections. Choose pebbles and slates that are long enough to be wedged in at least 2.5cm/1in below the surface of the "rug".

AFTERCARE

Protect the "rug" for three days by covering it with a board raised on bricks then overlaid by plastic sheeting. Avoid walking on the "rug" for at least a month to allow the mortar to cure fully.

Tools and Materials

- spade
- fine aggregate to fill the area to a depth of 10cm/4in
- cement
- watering can
- selection of pebbles, pieces of slate, terracotta pots, china ginger-jar pot lids
- tile nippers
- sharp sand
- mortar colour
- straight edge
- hammer
- soft brush
- board to cover rug area
- 4 bricks
- plastic sheeting

1 Prepare the mortar bedding by mixing equal quantities of sharp sand and cement. Add the mortar colour and mix in well. The design is worked while the mortar mix is dry, to enable you to change it if necessary. But the whole design must be completed in a day because moisture from the atmosphere will begin to set the mortar.

2 Pour the dry mix on to the flat bed and, using a straight edge, smooth it out until it is level with the rest of the paving. Then remove a small quantity of the mix from the centre so that it does not overflow as you work. This extracted mix can be put back at a later stage as required, as the design begins to take shape.

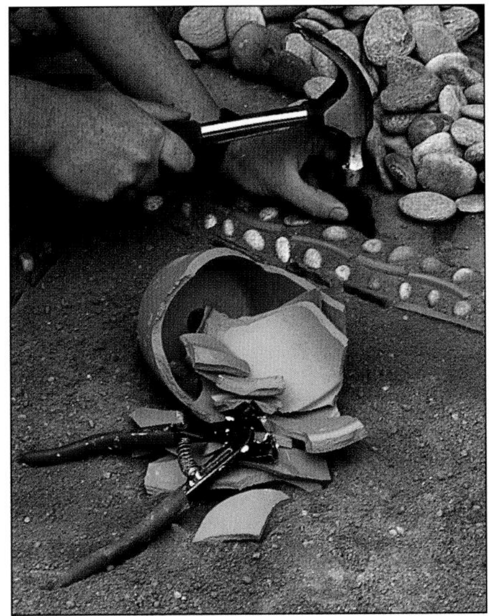

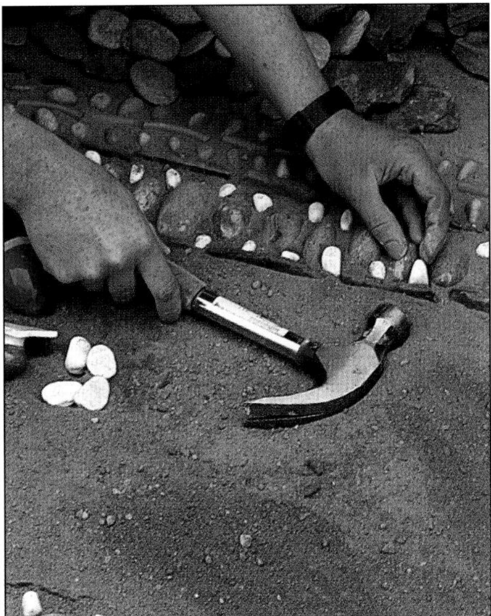

3 Plan the border design by arranging the pebbles, slates and the rim sections from the terracotta pots around the outside edge of the "rug" until you have a level, decorative border design. Working inwards, gently hammer the pieces into place.

4 Brush the mortar over the worked areas to make sure any gaps are filled. To build up the border design, continue working towards the centre, carefully hammering in the pebbles, slates and terracotta. Use china pot lids to add splashes of colour to the four corners.

5 Plan the design using the terracotta bases, pebbles and slate. Make sure the central area of mortar is level. Using tile nippers, cut the pieces of terracotta to size, then gently hammer everything into position. When the pattern is complete, brush the mortar around the decoration and use a watering can to dampen the surface. As the mortar absorbs the moisture, it will set hard.

Miniature Pebble Circle

Here is a very simple mosaic made from pieces of slate and old flower pots, plus a few beach pebbles, which can be used as a decorative detail anywhere in the garden.

Tools and Materials

- spade
- 16 brick pavers
- 5kg/11lb bag ready-mixed sand and cement
- mortar trowel
- slates
- terracotta crocks
- pebbles

1 Prepare a smooth circular area in the garden. Lay the pavers so that they radiate outwards, leaving the central area free. How far you extend the pavers will depend on the size of your prepared area.

2 Add sufficient water to the sand and cement mix to achieve a crumbly consistency. Using a mortar trowel, smooth the cement into the circle.

3 Working quickly before the cement sets, press in a border of slates, setting them on edge.

4 Working in concentric rings, add a circle of terracotta crocks and another of slates, then add a "wheel" of pebbles and terracotta.

■ OPPOSITE
Include this pebble circle as a decorative panel in a paved or gravelled area of the garden, or include it in a herb bed.

■ RIGHT
Try to include at least three different materials in the circle, as contrasting colours add interest to the design.

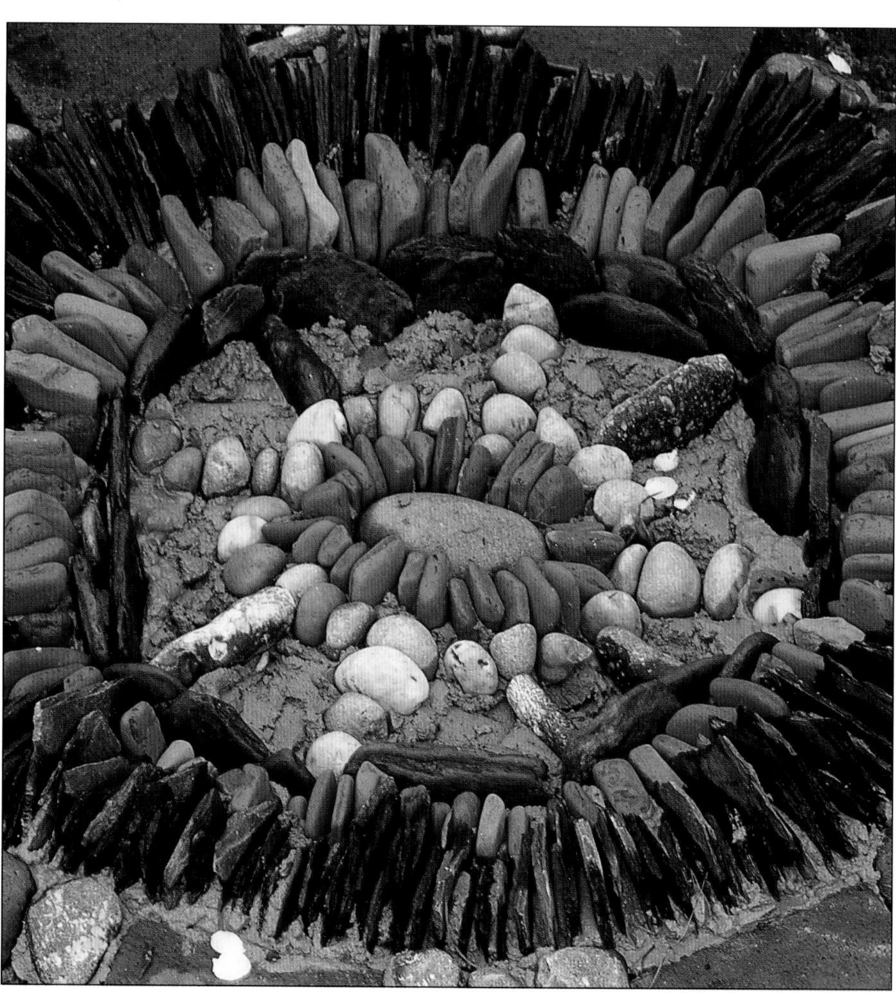

Mosaic Slabs

These large-scale pebble mosaics are very hardwearing and can be repeated as many times as necessary to lay as part of a path or patio. The square slab measures 36cm/14in across – anything larger becomes too unwieldy and will be more likely to break.

■ RIGHT
Sort your collection of pebbles by colour and shape to make decorative slabs with regular patterns. Using smaller frames, you can also create little pebble pictures to set in a floor or wall.

Tools and Materials

- selection of pebbles
- large sheet of paper
- hammer
- nails
- 4 38cm/15in lengths of 5 x 2.5cm/2 x 1in wood
- plastic sheet
- rubber gloves
- cement
- large bucket

1 Lay out the design first on a piece of paper the same size as the finished slab. Nail together the four pieces of wood to make a square frame.

2 Cover with a plastic sheet and put the frame in the centre. Wearing rubber gloves, mix the cement in a bucket and fill the frame.

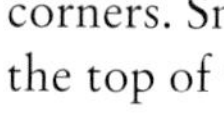

3 Use your hands to press the cement down firmly, especially into the corners. Smooth the surface just below the top of the frame.

4 Transfer the pebbles from the paper on to the cement, pressing each firmly in place. Leave for several days to allow the cement to set.

5 Remove the slab from the frame by banging the edge of the frame firmly on a hard surface. Repeat to make as many slabs as you need.

DECKING

Timber decking is a flexible material to work with, both in terms of actual installation and in how it is treated afterwards, as its appearance can be varied with wood stains or paint. It can also be used with other materials such as paving and gravel to give interesting textural variations.

■ ABOVE
Whitening wood, whether with bleach or a pale woodwash, accentuates the natural grain and gives it a lovely weathered, seaside look, as if it has been exposed to years of sunshine.

Decking is a surface associated with hot, dry climates, and it will give your garden a warm, sunny feel. In fact, it can also be used in wetter, colder areas as long as the timber is pressure-treated first.

On level or gently sloping ground, decking is not difficult to construct. Begin by mortaring rows of bricks on to a concrete

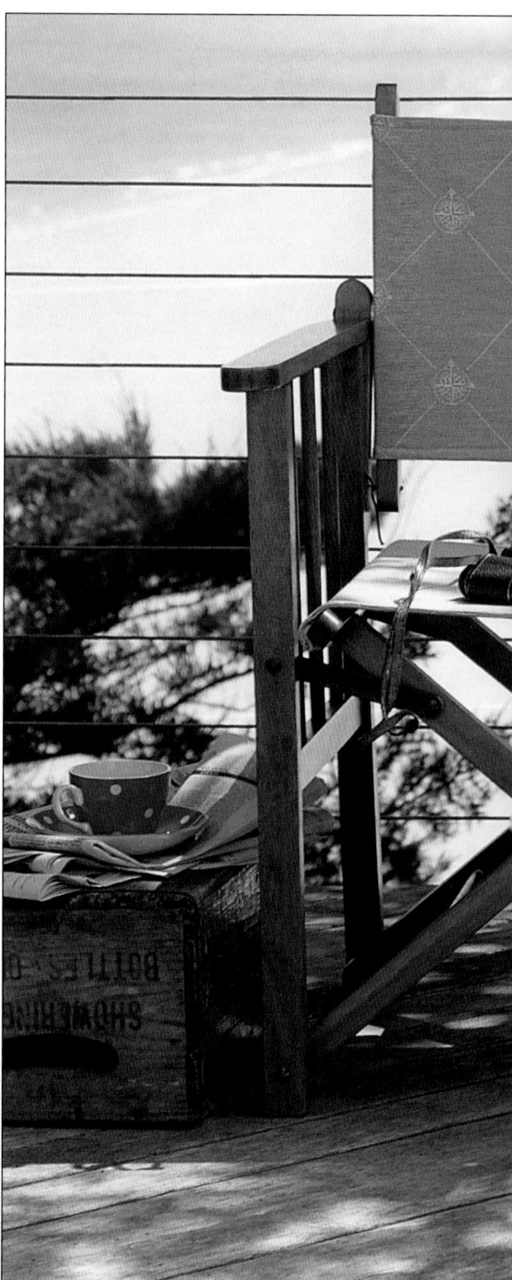

■ RIGHT
Timber decking and a metal rail are the perfect choice for a raised patio overlooking a marine view, giving the terrace a nautical feel. Laying the timbers diagonally, as here, has the effect of visually enlarging a small area.

foundation at right-angles to the intended direction of the decking and about 40cm/16in apart. Lay wooden joists along the rows of bricks, including a waterproof membrane such as plastic sheeting between the bricks and the joists. Screw the planks to the joists, and face the edges of the deck with lengths of timber. Allow narrow gaps between the boards to give free drainage and to allow for expansion in the wood.

Small, slatted panels are available ready-made from timber merchants and can be laid on compacted soil or gravel to make paths as well as patios. Lay them in alternate directions to give a checkerboard effect over a large area.

Reclaimed wood in the form of disused railway sleepers (ties) is very stable and will make a secure timber surface simply laid on compacted gravel. Sleepers have many uses in the garden: use them for edging borders and making raised flower beds, as well as for edging pathways and steps, to give the garden a unified appearance.

WALLS: THE GARDEN FRAMEWORK

It is the garden walls – and the plants and decorations you dress them with – that welcome visitors at eye level. So make your boundaries a vibrant part of your garden design, using colour, texture, pictures and decorations.

Garden walls and fences are essentially functional. They are there to define the boundaries, to keep children and pets safely within and intruders out. Nevertheless, they also fulfil a design function, affording the garden its main vertical structure. Depending on the circumstances, this can be emphasized or played down. The obvious example for most houses is the contrast between the front and back gardens. At the front, fences are usually low or visually lightweight, creating a boundary without obscuring the house to provide an open, welcoming look. At the back, however, the boundaries are more likely to be solid walls or fences to provide privacy from neighbouring gardens. They also form the background against which the garden can be planned. For this reason, the walls shouldn't be too dominant in themselves.

■ BELOW
An arched rose garland and mature border shrubs have created natural walls down the length of this garden path.

■ BELOW
Slow-growing topiary hedges lend an air of solid formality and neatness to any garden scene.

■ ABOVE
Well-established borders and hedges can be trained to form archways, framing paths and providing superb impact.

■ RIGHT
Foxgloves and trailing leaves cloak an old bent brick wall, lending it an informal and welcoming look.

■ BELOW
Climbing honeysuckle helps make a feature of this tumbling-down wall.

BOUNDARY CHOICES

The most appealing garden walls are those of well-seasoned brick, evocative as they are of the walled gardens that are integral to large country houses. They lend an air of permanence, have a pleasing crumbly texture and, because they retain and reflect heat, they can create a protected micro-climate within the garden. Garden walls look best built with local materials – stone, flint or local stock brick. If you are building or repairing a wall, seek out these local materials, as they will blend perfectly with the wall's setting.

■ OPPOSITE
Clambering yellow roses make a summer decoration, taking over from a spring flowering of wisteria.

■ BELOW
Crossed rustic poles bring decorous restraint to unruly rose shrubs.

PLANTED WALLS

As an alternative to hard materials, the plants themselves will also make effective garden "walls". Box and privet offer classic hedging that is very appealing and provides a rich green boundary all the year round. Hedges can be clipped into simple topiary shapes, which look just as good in small urban gardens as they do in larger rural ones. The trick is to keep them to the scale of the garden and its surroundings. Elaborate peacocks look fantastic in the country but, in urban situations, a neat orb or stately obelisk is more appropriate.

Larger conifers, such as thuja, can also provide lofty verdant hedging, which is perfect for protecting your privacy in built-up areas. However, some conifers will eventually grow very tall – up to 15m/50ft – so make sure you buy one of the more manageable varieties, such as *Thuja* 'Lutea nana', which stops at a modest height of about 1.8m/6ft, or 'Rheingold', which reaches 3–3.5m/10–12ft.

Another way of creating a living wall is to fix a trellis on which to grow climbers and ramblers. The classic choices are roses, honeysuckle, jasmine, clematis and the potato vine, *Solanum crispum*

or *S. jasminoides*, all of which produce flowers, for a fabulous floral wall. Cleverly painted, they can be combined to provide colour interest all year round. If your horticultural knowledge stops short of the encyclopaedic, plan your planting the easy way, by buying a new climber in flower every two or three months. They will all come up again the following year, ensuring another lovely display of seasonal colour.

More open plan screening can be provided by low walls teamed with low hedging. Again, the traditional box or privet will work well, or you can plant a pretty floral hedge, such as lavender or fuchsia – both of which will impart a beautiful fragrance over the garden.

WOOD AND METAL

As a non-planting option, wood is an ever-popular boundary choice, and will require very little upkeep once it is in place. Traditional picket fencing looks wonderful in classic clean white, or it can be painted to complement the plants. In country districts, rustic poles look good, especially if you don't want to obscure a wonderful view. Position them either upright in lines or arranged in a series of long, low crosses to create a loose trellis.

Metal is another hardwearing material for boundary dividers. Railings, marching regimentally across the front garden, look very smart in a city, while ornamental metal lattice or trellis produce a decorative effect almost anywhere.

■ BELOW

Metal railings are the classic smart answer for front gardens in town, but they are just as pleasing when used to enclose a rambling country plot. Their appeal is the precise, military line they draw that unequivocally says "no entry" without obstructing the view.

■ LEFT
This living wall of roses makes a delightful garden boundary. Even grown over quite a flimsy framework of trellis or chain link, roses soon thicken into dense cover, which protects your privacy as much as any more solid planting.

■ BELOW
A high brick wall is effective at keeping out visitors but can be monotonous on the eye. Growing reliable climbers, such as clematis and rose, will help minimize the repetition of the brickwork.

■ ABOVE

This white climbing rose overhangs the roof of an outbuilding and acts as a natural barrier, preventing intruders and protecting the privacy of the garden. Blooming foliage always looks magnificent, especially when it is used to enhance an existing garden structure.

FENCES

Fencing, wooden or otherwise, makes the ideal boundary choice when privacy is not the priority – such as at the front of the house, where you may prefer to be a little more open and welcoming while still needing a clear definition of your boundary.

The most common garden boundaries consist of wooden lapped fencing, which is relatively inexpensive to buy and very quick and easy to put up. Wooden fencing can be bought in panels, ready-treated against rot, and is nailed or screwed to posts, which can be fixed into "collars" of long metal spikes, firmly driven into the ground. A similarly solid-looking boundary is wattle fencing. Woven from young willow branches, this traditional fencing dates back to the Bronze Age in Britain. With its bark intact, the wattle provides a very attractive fine texture against which plants can grow and clamber. Wattle fencing is available as "hurdles" (panels) of various widths and heights, and it is erected in much the same way as more commonplace wooden fencing.

■ BELOW
Picket fencing makes for a simple but efficient boundary, which can be left plain or painted to match a colour scheme.

■ ABOVE
White-painted picket fencing provides a classic boundary marker that is perenially pleasing. The crisp, uniform line of wooden posts, with its picot edging at the top, provides a framework to the garden that looks smart wherever you live.

Entrances and Exits

Depending on where they are, garden gates and doors have different functions and a different decorative appeal. Front gates welcome visitors, directing them towards the front door, and like front fences are generally lower and more screen-like in appearance. Gates and doors at the side of the garden and leading into the back serve quite the opposite purpose, that of protecting against intruders, and are generally more solid.

The entrance and exit each have their own role in the visual design of the garden. They offer a break in the possible monotony of a wall and, since their presence suggests that they lead somewhere, they can also lend an intriguing extra dimension to the garden. Even if it doesn't actually go anywhere, a door in a wall or fence gives the romantic impression of leading to a hidden garden or unknown space. A solid back gate also allows a feeling of privacy: in the garden, you are in a secret place, accessible only to those you allow in.

■ OPPOSITE
A half-hidden exquisite, weathered wood and metal door makes a highly decorative garden entrance.

■ BELOW
A discreet basket in full bloom hangs beside an old garden storeroom door, and acts as an enticement to visitors passing through the garden.

■ ABOVE
This tall, metal gate leads from one part of the garden to another, lending intrigue to a space that would have offered less interest had it been one large open area.

■ ABOVE
This ordinary garden door made of wooden slats looks altogether more inviting with the addition of a simple twig wreath, which was made from materials found in the garden.

Trelliswork

Trellis is a great garden material. It can be used as a wall in itself, providing a framework for climbers and ramblers. It can be used as a divider within the garden to lend perspective, and to add height to walls where extra privacy is needed. It can also be used to decorate the walls themselves. The decorative aspect is especially valuable when walls or fences are less than beautiful, or where you would like to add a little extra texture.

■ BELOW
A fabulous Indian metal trellis panel makes an imaginative framework for a special feature. The frame has been painted in verdigris colours, and pale blue urns, planted with *saxifrage*, complete the picture.

The trellis does not have to be ready-made. Old gates, an old window frame without the glass, metal panels or panels made from grape vine stems and other organic materials can all serve the same purpose as ordinary trelliswork. They all have the advantage of looking good even before the climbers have been planted. More traditional trelliswork can be given a head start with a lick of paint, which immediately gives it a more finished and individual appearance.

■ ABOVE
An old wrought-iron gate provides an elegant trellis framework for a miniature climbing rose.

■ RIGHT
Here, painted square trellis has been used as a screen, dividing off one part of the garden. It provides an excellent framework for a climbing rose and clematis. This trellis can also be a pretty solution for a boundary fence.

■ BELOW
Evocative, organic twig trellis panels make a wonderful frame for a montage of climbing roses and additional decorative features such as twiggy stars and metal lanterns.

Adding Colour

Inside the house, once the walls are plastered, you immediately think about decorating them. Outside, people are still a little frightened of colour, preferring to play safe by sticking to the natural tones of stone, brick and wood. In a decorative garden, colour is very important. Not only can the paint you choose suggest mood and ambience, just as it does inside, it can also be used to emphasize the colour scheme of the garden planting.

■ BELOW
Sugar-almond shades differentiate two properties. In the far garden, the pastel pink perfectly matches the climbing rose growing inside the picket fence.

The surfaces you paint may be the house walls, walls of outside buildings such as garages or sheds, or they may be the garden boundary walls. Maybe you have a mixture of fencing and trelliswork, all of slightly different woods and ages, that has resulted in a visual muddle. A coat of weatherproof emulsion (latex) will make all the difference: giving the fixtures all the same decorative finish will produce a much more coherent look for the whole garden.

Or you may have newly erected trelliswork that has a year or more to wait for a verdant covering of creepers. Giving it a coat of paint when you put it up means you will have some attractive colour to look at while the plants grow.

Colour can be used to single out one area of the garden. You can pinpoint the features destined for a particular colour scheme, or you may wish to highlight the planting.

Painted fences and surfaces give year-round colour to the garden and are particularly valuable in winter when many of the plants have died down. This is the ideal time to give fences and gates a fresh coat of paint. Unlike interior decoration, you don't need to spend a lot of time on preparation. There is no need to fill holes or sand down. Just scrub the wood down with warm water to clean it, and allow it to dry thoroughly before applying the paint. If you plan to paint an outdoor house wall, however, you will usually need to apply a primer to the clean and dry wall surface before adding your chosen colour.

■ BELOW LEFT
Colour can be used to transform any of the objects in your garden, and whether the change is permanent or temporary, the effect is the same. Here, a potting shed has been enlivened in an afternoon simply by painting the otherwise plain bins in bright shades of green.

■ BELOW
This window sill edged with brilliant ceramic tiles adds vibrant colour, which is matched in summer by a row of red pelargoniums.

Paint and Wall Options

Nobody would dream of painting a beautiful old stone or brick wall, but if your walls are made of more modern materials they may be less sympathetic to the rest of the garden, or just look dull or grimy. If your fencing is the popular panelled variety, it is likely to arrive coated in a protective preservative, usually a violent shade of rust that you will want to cover up quickly. A coat of paint is the quickest way to bring light and brightness into the shadiest garden, and to add colour that is not seasonal.

There's no need to limit yourself to a single colour when painting a wall or a row of fencing. Paint your wall and cover it with trellis painted in a contrasting colour, or paint the wall in stripes or bold blocks of colour, adding smaller designs using stencils.

And if in a year or two you have changed your mind about your design, or if the planting scheme has changed, just paint it again.

■ OPPOSITE
A decorative edge in stripes of bright Caribbean colours gives life to a plain white wall and door. Masking tape was used to keep the lines straight and, when they were all complete and dry, the leaves were added using a stencil.

■ BELOW LEFT
Three colours of paint have been used to brighten this outdoor setting. Such a bold use of colour, intensified by a vibrant display of plants on the wall and cushions in primary shades, gives the corner a strong Mediterranean feel.

■ BELOW
Don't be put off by thinking white walls look cold and bare in anything but a tropical climate. This brightly painted door adds some positive colour, and is itself offset by the white. The addition of the electric lamp completes the picture of a very smart doorway.

Ideas with Paint

Whether you want to paint your garden wall, or a house wall that faces the garden, there is plenty of inspiration to be had. Experiment not only with colour but with technique.

As well as straight colour, you can create depth by layering the colours. Try trompe l'oeil effects such as marble, stone, slate or moss. Stencil designs on to walls, use potato prints, geometric designs or even simple motifs. The trick is to consider the scale. These effects will have to be seen from much further away than they would if used indoors. Even a 9m/30ft garden is much larger than the average room, so everything has to be exaggerated a little. Paint effects need to be a little less subtle, and motifs generally larger.

■ RIGHT
This sunny yellow wall was given a rough-textured look by trowelling on a ready-mixed medium (joint compound), available from DIY (hardware) stores. Colourwashing in two shades of yellow gives depth and tone.

■ FAR RIGHT
Give new shutters or doors a weatherworn look by applying wax between two layers of different-coloured paint. The colours used here are creamy yellow beneath bright blue.

■ ABOVE
A checkerboard pattern always makes a striking display and is a traditional design in many communities, so it is unlikely to date. This one in tan and cream was inspired by African decoration; the same design in china blue and white would evoke Provence. The design doesn't necessarily have to be neat and even; as here, little irregularities add to its charm. If you trust your eye, paint it freehand, using a fine brush to create the outline of each square and then filling it in with colour. If you would prefer something a little more orderly, cut a large square stencil and position it on the wall. Cover a whole wall if you are feeling adventurous, or simply work the design on window and door reveals and along skirting areas.

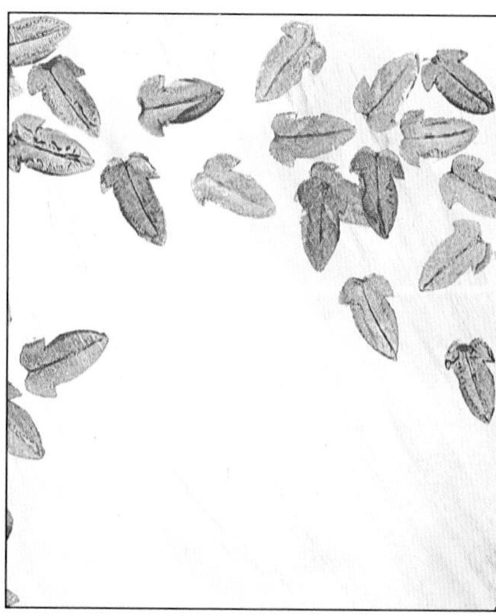

■ ABOVE
This cascade of falling leaves was created using a potato print, which can be just as effective outside as in. Choose a simple motif, like this oak leaf, and, using the point of a knife, gently "draw" the outline on to the cut surface of half a large potato. Cut away the potato from around the outline to a depth of about 9mm/⅜in and "draw" in the veins. Give the wall a pale colourwash base. When that has fully dried, dip the potato into a stronger colour of paint, stamp it on a piece of newspaper to remove the excess paint, then stamp on to the wall.

■ ABOVE
Marbling makes the perfect effect for an outside wall, since it works best in oil-based paints that are ideal for outside use. It should be applied to a smooth surface. The veins are applied over a paint base while it is still wet, and splashes of white spirit (turpentine) are added to soften the hard edges.

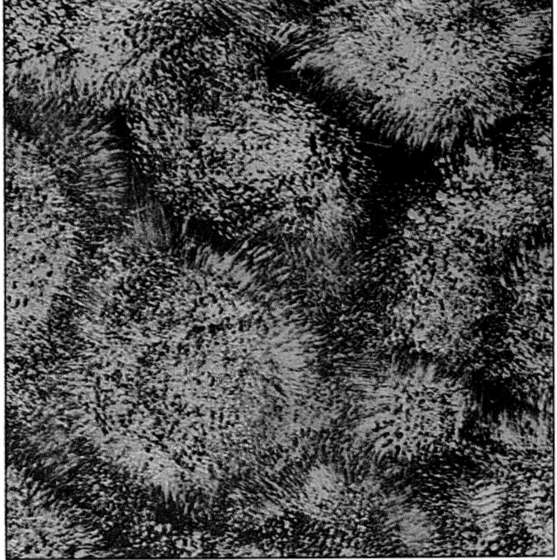

■ ABOVE
Evocative of the sunny Mediterranean, lemons and limes make wonderful motifs that anyone can manage. Cut a stencil or paint them freehand. Paint the shapes randomly like this or make a trompe d'oeil by painting a simple shelf of plates decorated with lemons.

■ ABOVE
An unprepossessing garden or shed wall gives the impression of having the patina of time when stippled in shades of green to give a mossed effect. First apply a colourwash of mid- to dark green, then roll on a pale green and, finally, stipple on some ochre with the tip of the brush.

■ ABOVE
Naive lizard-like animal motifs are traditional in many cultures. This one, inspired by African art, is not dissimilar to motifs used by Native Americans. Just one lizard in the corner of a sunny wall would transform it from the ordinary to something special.

Decorative Garden Fixtures and Fittings

It is the fixtures and fittings you choose for your garden that help determine your theme. A water feature conveys a tranquil mood, while a brightly-painted play house and a pirate ship built from a tree will make the garden a children's paradise of fairy-tale adventure.

There are a multitude of choices for garden fixtures. Dividers in the form of arches, arbours and pergolas partition your space, with plants trained over and around the structure to soften the impact of the wood or metal materials from which the divider is made. Clever tricks with wood stains and paint will help solve the problem of an unsightly garden shed. The secret is to look at your immovable garden fixtures in a new way, and transform them into features which will contribute an extra architectural dimension to your garden design.

■ ABOVE
Garden paraphernalia has a charm all of its own.

■ OPPOSITE
The trellis arbour offers a sheltered place in the garden for chatting, reading or just quiet contemplation.

Dividers and Arches

Even the smallest garden can accommodate fixtures such as arches, arbours, pergolas and trellis screens and still have room for a small garden shed or play house. And while the hard landscaping and planted borders will dictate the layout of the garden, it is these vertical elements that greatly affect its structure and overall look.

Vertical structures such as pergolas and garden buildings can be positioned around the garden's perimeter to give shape, while rose arches, walkways and trellis screens can be used as dividers. Anything that divides the garden lends extra perspective because it defines another space, and even in gardens that are fairly limited in size, being able to glimpse beyond into another area creates the illusion of greater space. An arch that forms the entrance to the garden is a particularly successful feature as it governs the visitor's initial impression of the garden, framing the scene beyond and creating interest and atmosphere.

TRELLIS

If you want to screen off part of the garden – to define an eating area, perhaps, or to section off a vegetable garden – the simplest solution is to use trellis, which is wonderfully versatile and comes in a variety of panel shapes and sizes. As well as the basic rectangular panels, there are panels with pointed, convex or concave tops and even with integral "windows", all of which provide plenty of scope for creativity. When it comes to the finishing touches, there is a wide choice of attractive finials in shapes such as globes, acorns, pineapples and obelisks, which can be used as additional decoration.

ARCHES

If you prefer not to screen off a whole area to lend perspective, a rose arch can have the desired effect. Buy a ready-made metal arch or make a simple wooden one using pergola posts. Another option is to use plants, planting young trees either side of a path, and tying them at the top so that they grow into an arch. Remember to make the arch wide enough to get through when it is fully clad with plants, and don't use plants with thorny stems if they are likely to brush against people walking under the arch. The rose 'Zéphirine Drouhin' is an excellent choice as it is thornless.

■ LEFT
Rustic poles fixed horizontally to wooden pillars form a kind of trellis that makes an ideal support for a climbing rose such as 'Felicia', and still works well as a garden divider in winter when the rose is not in bloom.

Climbers for Arches

Akebia quinata (chocolate vine)
Campsis radicans (trumpet vine)
Clematis
Humulus (hop)
Lonicera (honeysuckle)
Rosa (roses)
Vigna caracalla (climbing bean)
Vitis (grape vines)

■ RIGHT
Beautiful walkways can be created by training foliage to grow over metal arches. Here, the light covering of leaves lets in dappled sunlight along the length of the path, providing the perfect setting for a pleasant early evening stroll.

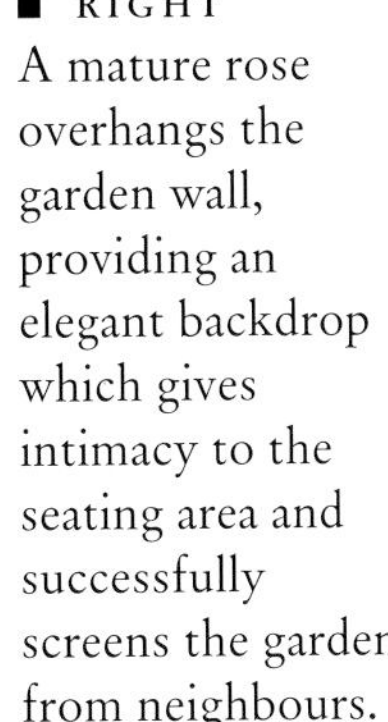

■ RIGHT
A mature rose overhangs the garden wall, providing an elegant backdrop which gives intimacy to the seating area and successfully screens the garden from neighbours.

WALKWAYS, PERGOLAS AND ARBOURS

As well as serving as a light screen, an arch can mark the beginning of a walkway. If you have enough space in the garden, a walkway has great appeal. There is something peaceful and cloister-like about a walk beneath a leafy tunnel through which natural light filters to the ground. Even in a small garden, a simple, verdant archway offers a sense of romantic adventure – the idea of going somewhere – and it needn't cut into too much garden space.

WALKWAYS

Walkways can be as simple as an elongated archway – probably the best option in a small garden – or a long snaking affair down one side of the garden. They can be made from metal or from wooden poles forming a series of arches. The effect of a walkway can be made even more powerful if punctuated at the end by a focal point in the classical style. In a formal garden, this may all have been planned as part of the landscaping, the walkway leading perhaps to a door or gateway or an exquisite piece of garden statuary. But you can adapt the idea for a more modest setting and still create impact. A specimen plant or a favourite pot or container, beautifully planted up, will provide a satisfying focal point at the end of the walkway, while acquiring a greater sense of importance for itself as it attracts the attention of everyone who strolls there.

■ ABOVE
This pagoda-topped metal walkway lends an almost oriental feel to the garden. Beautiful old Greek pithoi set in a bed of vibrant euphorbias and hellebores are used to great effect as the focal point at the end.

■ ABOVE
Wonderful cascades of laburnum make a flamboyant golden walkway.

PERGOLAS

Pergolas are first cousins to walkways, being covered areas often fixed on to one side of the house. These work well in all sizes of garden, providing an attractive, natural, covered outdoor "room" and serving as a transition area between inside and out. They make delightful shady outdoor eating areas that afford extra privacy from overlooking neighbours.

ARBOURS

Leafy arbours lend architectural form to a garden while taking up very little space. Tucked against a wall, an arbour will create structure in even the smallest garden, offering somewhere shady to sit, relax and read or chat with a friend. At its simplest, an arbour could be formed by training climbing plants up a wall to form an arch over a garden bench, though it is not difficult to make a more permanent structure.

■ RIGHT
The large overhanging fig (*Ficus carica*) and the surrounding rose, clematis and other climbers growing on this house wall have created an intimate setting for the table and chairs, which fulfils all the functions of an arbour even though there is no supporting structure.

■ LEFT
Flanked by greenery and shaded overhead by a roof of honeysuckle, this delightful arbour is set against the fabulous texture of a brick and flint wall. By incorporating the existing structure of the garden, it takes on an authentic "lived-in" feel. The weathered, rustic wooden bench and table are left out throughout the year, offering further structure to this part of the garden.

Trellis Arbour

An arbour is one of the easiest ways to introduce architectural structure to even the smallest of gardens, and it is no more difficult to make one than it is to put up a fence. This arbour is made up of trellis panels, painted with an outdoor stain in a cool, deep colour to tone with the bench. The result is an enchanting, original bower.

1 Gather together the trellis panels and "dry assemble" them to ensure that you are happy with the design. Two of the 1.8m x 60cm/6 x 2ft panels are for the sides and the third is for the top. The two narrow panels and the concave panel form the front and the 1.8m x 90cm/6 x 3ft panel is to be used horizontally at the top of the back. Trim the wooden posts to length: they should measure 1.8m/6ft plus the depth of the metal "shoe" at the top of the post support.

Tools and Materials

- lattice (diagonal) trellis panels in the following sizes:
- 3 panels 1.8m x 60cm/6 x 2ft
- 2 panels 1.8m x 30cm/6 x 1ft
- 1 concave panel 1.8m x 46cm/6 x 1½ft
- 1 panel 1.8m x 90cm/6 x 3ft
- 6 timber posts 7.5 x 7.5cm/3 x 3in, each 2.1m/7ft long
- saw
- 6 spiked metal post supports, 7.5 x 7.5cm/3 x 3in, each 75cm/2½ft long
- mallet
- 10 x 5cm/2in galvanized nails
- hammer
- electric drill with No 8 bit and screwdriver attachment
- 40 x 3cm/1¼in No 10 zinc-coated steel screws
- 2.5 litre/½ gallon can exterior woodstain
- paintbrush

2 Start with the back panel. The posts need to be placed 1.8m/6ft apart. Mark their positions, then, using a mallet, drive in a spiked metal post on each side. Drive a trimmed post into each of the metal "shoes". Using galvanized nails, temporarily fix the top of the trellis to the top of the posts. Using a No 8 bit, drill holes for the screws at intervals down each side of the trellis and screw the panel to the posts.

3 In the same way, position the outside front posts and fix the side panels, then the inside front posts and front panels. Fix the concave panel into the panels either side of it. Finally, fix the roof in position, screwing it into the posts. Paint the arbour with exterior woodstain and leave to dry.

■ RIGHT
Diagonal trellis makes a picturesque arbour for a garden seat even before climbing plants have had time to scramble over it. To soften its lines while it is new, you can provide extra decoration with hanging baskets and plants in containers.

GARDEN STRUCTURES

Any kind of building adds to the framework of the garden and there are few gardens that don't have at least one, be it a garden shed, summer house or play house. They are usually left just as they were when they were put up, but it is never too late to turn them into decorative features in their own right.

A garden shed can be transformed with paint – in pale, pretty stripes like a beach hut, for example – or it can be given a more substantial-looking roof of slates. Climbers can be grown up garden buildings. Play houses can be decorated to give them a fairy-tale appeal. Honeysuckle or clematis can be grown over the roof and hanging baskets hung from the eaves.

Follies were a favourite in the gardens of Victorian homes, built in fanciful styles from Gothic to oriental. It is not difficult to incorporate fun in the form of a folly – a Gothic shed, pagoda or temple. These can be bought ready to put up, or you could scour architectural salvage yards for attractive doors and windows to incorporate in a new design.

■ ABOVE
Architectural salvage, some pillars and posts, plenty of imagination and clever use of paint make an eyecatching latter-day garden folly.

■ LEFT
If you find you can put a dreary garden shed to better use, remove the doors and add seating to build yourself a charming retreat, and to make the most of an existing structure in your garden.

■ OPPOSITE
This delightful gazebo is made from a simple metal frame overgrown with climbers. The bench seating was built around the supporting wooden joist in the centre.

Decorating a Shed

Even the most unpromising garden buildings can be turned into something special. When this one was "inherited" with the garden, it was little more than a concrete block. With the addition of some paint and plaster shapes, available from architectural plaster suppliers, it took on the appearance of a miniature Mediterranean villa.

Tools and Materials

- pencil
- stiff paper
- scissors
- 1cm/½in MDF (medium-density fiberboard)
- jigsaw or fretsaw
- acrylic wood primer
- decorator's and artist's paintbrushes
- emulsion (latex) paint in dark blue
- fine-textured masonry paint in white
- acrylic scumble glaze
- artist's acrylic paint in light blue, red, orange and yellow
- soft cloths
- nails
- hammer
- stiff brush
- palette knife
- exterior tile adhesive
- selection of small, ornamental plaster motifs
- electrical insulation tape
- panel pins (tacks)
- pliers
- natural sponge
- matt exterior polyurethane varnish

1 Draw a Moorish roof motif on a sheet of paper to fit the top of the door. Cut out and place this template on the MDF, drawing around the shape. Cut out using a jigsaw or fretsaw.

2 Paint both the door and the MDF panel with acrylic wood primer and allow to dry for 1–2 hours. Paint one coat of dark blue emulsion (latex) and allow to dry for 2–3 hours.

3 Mix up a glaze using fine-textured masonry paint and acrylic scumble glaze and add a little water to give the consistency of double (heavy) cream, then tint with light blue artist's acrylic. Paint the door and shaped panel, brushing in the direction of the grain.

4 Quickly wipe off the glaze using a soft cloth to knock back the colour and leave to dry. Nail the MDF panel to the top of the door, and paint the nail heads with the pale blue glaze.

5 Using a stiff brush, scrub the wall surfaces to remove the dirt. Use a palette knife to "butter" the back of each plaster motif with exterior tile adhesive and stick them to the wall. Use electrical insulation tape and panel pins (tacks) tapped into the wall under the shapes to hold the plaster shapes in position overnight while the adhesive dries.

6 Remove the tape and pins with pliers, then paint the wall with one coat of fine-textured masonry paint. Leave to dry for 4–6 hours.

7 Tint three pots of acrylic scumble glaze with artist's acrylic paints – one red, one orange and one yellow – and dilute to the consistency of single cream. Using a damp sponge, wipe the colours randomly on to the wall, blending the edges. Wipe off the excess with a cloth.

8 Using an artist's brush, stipple extra colour into any detailing to add emphasis. Leave the paint to dry for at least 4 hours, then varnish the wall.

■ ABOVE
The dull, cement-rendered walls of this old garden shed have been given a new vibrancy with a mix of hot Mediterranean colours and an assortment of finely detailed plaster ornaments clustered like a colony of exotic crustaceans.

Adding Wall Decorations

Once you are happy with the basic structure and colour of your garden walls, you can start to add more personal touches with the decorations. The most obvious garden decorations are wall-hung pots, sconces, brackets and small items of statuary. But almost any collection could find a home on the garden wall as long as it is weatherproof. Birdcages, birdfeeders, shells, lanterns and willow or wire wreaths can all be suspended on an outside wall. Or you could make a feature of wall-mounted shelves by filling them with pots, bottles and baskets, or with enamel or galvanized ware.

■ RIGHT
An outdoor lantern is a pretty wall decoration both day and night. This one has been decorated with a simple garland of twigs. For a party on a summer evening, it holds a thick church candle tucked into a terracotta pot, and is given a sparkling bow as a finishing touch.

■ OPPOSITE
A group of galvanized containers makes a shapely collection on a cottage wall, their wonderful, soft metal shades blending harmoniously with the garden.

■ BELOW
The elemental colours and textures of seashells make them the perfect foil for plants. A selection of shells have been used here to enhance a ready-made "window" in the garden wall.

Children's Play Fixtures

In family homes, gardens are very much for the children. They need their own outdoor space to play in, and where there isn't enough room to run or kick a ball the best solution is to set aside one area of the garden and build some sort of structure especially for them. They may like a play house, which provides for all-weather play, or they may prefer a climbing frame or a swing. If such structures are well planned, they need not take up too much space.

If you are lucky enough to have a suitable tree in your garden, you may be inspired to build a tree house, which won't take up any space in the garden at all. It is important to build a strong platform, distributing the load across as many branches as possible, and to surround it with a barrier. A temporary house can be made by suspending a tent from the branches above, or you can add walls, a roof and additional features to customize the house. You can also hang a swing from a branch (which should have a diameter of at least 15cm/6in to be strong enough). The best surface to lay under trees used for playing is chipped bark, which looks natural and is hardwearing yet soft enough to land on safely.

SAFETY FIRST

Whether you are buying play equipment for your children or building it yourself, it is important that it is strong, sturdy and steady, that wood is sanded smooth and that nails and screws are safely sunk below the surface. Ready-made equipment should conform to approved safety standards, and, once you have bought the items, everything should be checked and maintained regularly.

■ ABOVE
These steps up to a platform built around a tree lead to a slide. The same idea could be adapted for a tree house.

■ LEFT
Play houses can be decorated to enhance the whole garden. They not only offer a private place for imaginative play in the early years and a den as the children get older, but they also provide storage space for bulkier toys such as free-standing toy kitchens and dolls' houses.

■ RIGHT
A delightful little crooked house, complete with veranda and chimney, is built on stilts with a short stairway leading up to it. The very stuff of nursery stories, many an hour can be whiled away here in imaginative play.

■ BELOW
Climbing frames made from rustic poles blend happily into the garden. Carefully designed, they can be added to as children grow and develop their agility.

■ ABOVE
This well-constructed play house will provide at least five or six years' entertainment for a child. Most children love to have their own small garden plot to cultivate, and it makes good sense to site this just outside the play house. When the children have outgrown the house it can be turned into a potting shed.

■ ABOVE
If there is plenty of space in the garden, a climbing frame can be extended piece by piece to include swings, a slide, a rope ladder and a covered area that could easily double as a play house or look-out post.

■ RIGHT
A large, sturdy tree would be an asset in any garden, but is particularly useful in family gardens because of the potential it offers for children's play fixtures. A simple swing is easily assembled and will provide hours of fun for active children.

■ LEFT
In an average-sized garden a substantial climbing frame may well be the dominant feature, so it should be chosen for its looks as well as for its play value. This well-made wooden frame is nicely in keeping with the style of the garden.

■ ABOVE
A sandpit is one of the easiest pieces of play equipment to construct and then adapt later on. A lid is important to protect the sand from the weather and from cats. This timber decking lid makes an attractive feature in its own right.

■ ABOVE
A tree platform is good fun for older children and is simple to construct in a suitable tree, using sturdy wood off-cuts. Provide access via a rope ladder, which can be rolled up once the children are up.

Customized Play House

You can create an enchanting fairy-tale house that will add interest to the garden, while providing a play area the children will love. Give yourself a head start by buying one off the shelf and customizing it. Play houses usually come pre-treated against rot, which means they already have an excellent base for decoration (but do check this before you buy). This one has been given a slate roof with terracotta baby ridge tiles, shutters and a decorative fascia. The transformation is completed with a couple of coats of paint. This encompasses quite a few skills, so you might prefer to make things simpler for yourself by just painting the house in a range of cheerful colours.

FIXING THE ROOF SLATES

Work out how many slates (composition shingles) you need for each row. If the slates don't fit the width, place as many whole slates in the bottom row as it will take, then cut two equal strips to fill in at each end. Score and snap each slate in half widthways and secure in position by hammering nails through the pre-drilled holes into the roofing felt. The next row of slates will completely cover the first row of half slates. Arrange them so the side of each slate runs down the centre of the slate below. Nail in position. Position the third row so that the slates lie across the width, as for the first row. The bottom of the third row should line up with the top of the first row of half slates. Lay the fourth row like the second row, and so on.

FITTING THE SHUTTERS

Remove the window crossbars. If the shutters are larger than the window openings, cut the openings to fit using a hacksaw. Attach each shutter with a pair of hinges. Re-use the window bars as shutter stops and fit the door magnets in place.

DECORATING

Paint the play house with oil-based paint and allow to dry for at least 4 hours, or overnight, in fine weather. Then finish with a coat of polyurethane varnish.

ADDING THE RIDGE TILES

Mix up the sand and cement according to the manufacturer's instructions. Fill each end of each ridge tile with the mixture and "butter" some along the length of the ridge. Bed the tiles firmly into position and let dry.

ADDING THE FASCIA

Saw the fascia (bargeboard) to length, mitring the ends to match the angle of the roof in the centre. Paint the fascia with an oil-based paint and fix in place by pre-drilling pilot holes then nailing it to the front edge of the roof.

■ RIGHT
To transform a standard wooden play house into a child's dream cottage, add a few pieces of children's furniture to complete the home-sweet-home feel.

■ RIGHT
Plain wooden play houses can be difficult to accomodate visually with the rest of the garden. Painting and decorating the play house in a style sympathetic to the garden will help it fit in more easily.

Tools and Materials

- wooden play house
- mineral-fibre roof slates (composition shingles): enough to cover the roof plus half as much again
- craft knife
- metal straight edge
- 2 x 19mm/¾in nails per slate
- hammer
- 2 pairs louvred shutters to fit the windows (if the exact size is not available, choose a larger size and trim to fit)
- hacksaw
- 8 non-ferrous hinges
- 4 door magnets
- oil-based paint
- paintbrush
- baby ridge tiles to fit the length of the ridge
- ready-mixed sand and cement
- trowel
- decorative fascia (bargeboard) pre-cut from MDF (medium-density fiberboard)
- saw
- electric drill

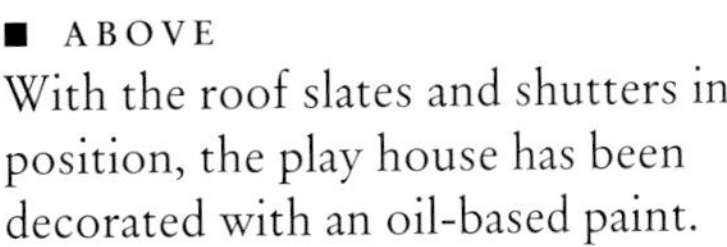

■ ABOVE
With the roof slates and shutters in position, the play house has been decorated with an oil-based paint.

■ ABOVE
The original window divides have been re-used as shutter stops and door magnets, fixed in place to hold the shutters closed.

HANGING PICTURES

Few walls inside the house are complete until the pictures are hung, and there is no reason why pictures should not be hung outside, too, although they will obviously need to be weatherproof. Ceramic tiled panels, mosaics, old enamel advertisements and painted wood panels all make excellent outdoor pictures.

■ RIGHT
A quirky, ceramic mosaic face smiles out from a curtain of ivy.

■ BELOW
A ceramic tile plaque echoes the colours of the painted garden seat and overflowing wisteria.

Wall Mosaic Picture

A wall mosaic in the garden can afford to be quite playful, peering out from its leafy surroundings. This contemplative princess is made up flat on a board and then moved as a whole to be fixed to the wall. The picture uses glass mosaic tiles in vibrant colours, secured to the board with glue, which will not fade when exposed to the elements.

1 Draw the design on craft paper and lay on a board. Make a tracing of the outline and cut out to act as a template when transferring the design to the wall.

3 Cut pink vitreous glass tiles into quarters and glue them face down to fill between the outlines. Cut the mirror into quarters and glue on to the dress and crown. Cut the tiles for the dress and crown into quarters and stick face down between the mirror pieces. When dry, carry the mosaic to the wall on the board. Draw around the template on the wall and fill the area with cement-based adhesive. Press on the mosaic, paper side up, and let dry for 2 hours. Dampen the paper and peel away. Leave to dry overnight. Grout with cement-based adhesive. Clean off any excess cement and let dry. Rub gently with sandpaper and polish with a soft cloth.

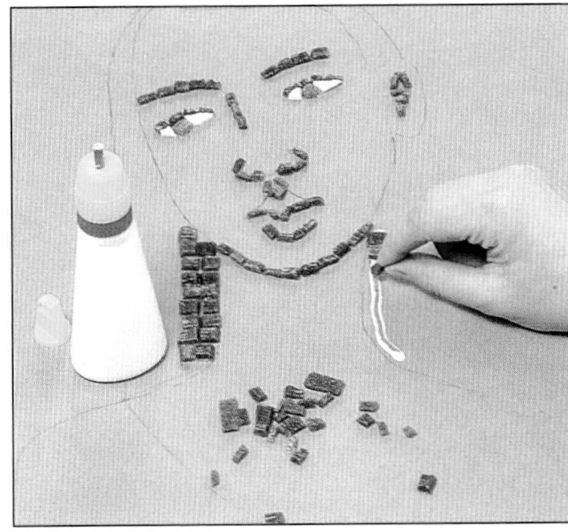

2 Cut the tiles for the outline into eighths, using tile nippers, and stick them face down on to the main lines of your drawing using water-soluble glue. Add key features to the face, such as eyes and lips, in contrasting colours.

■ BELOW
Brilliant glass mosaic with fragments of sparkling mirror will catch the light, and the eye, glinting from a garden wall.

Tools and Materials

- pencil
- brown craft paper
- board
- tracing paper
- scissors
- vitreous glass mosaic tiles, including pink tiles
- tile nippers
- water-soluble glue
- mirror
- cement-based tile adhesive
- flexible (putty) knife
- sponge
- sandpaper
- soft cloth

Garden Mosaic Panel

This richly textured panel is composed of tesserae cut from patterned china. Motifs are cut out and used as focal points for the patterns, and some of them are raised to give emphasis. The panel is worked on a plywood base to create a three-dimensional effect on the wall. This means that it can be assembled while lying flat, then hung from a hook like a picture.

Tools and Materials

- pencil
- 2cm/¾in plywood
- jigsaw
- sandpaper
- PVA (white) glue
- paintbrushes
- wood primer
- undercoat
- gloss paint
- mirror plate
- drill and rebate bit
- 2cm/¾in screw
- screwdriver
- ruler, set square or compasses (optional)
- selection of old china
- tile nippers
- tile adhesive
- powdered tile grout
- cement dye
- rubber gloves
- squeegee or flexible (putty) knife
- nailbrush
- soft cloth

1 Draw the shape of the panel on the plywood. Cut out the shape using a jigsaw and sand the edges. Seal the front and edges of the panel with diluted PVA (white) glue. Paint the back with wood primer, undercoat and gloss paint – let each coat dry before applying the next.

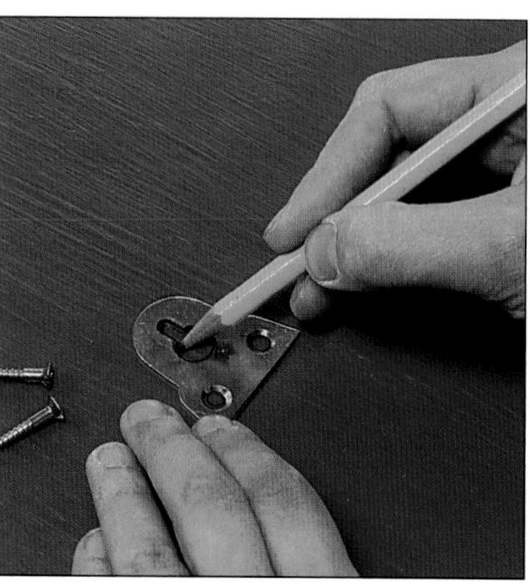

2 Mark the position of the mirror plate on the back of the panel. Drill out the area under the keyhole opening large enough to take a screw head. Screw the mirror plate in position.

3 Draw your design on the sealed top surface. Tools such as a ruler, set square and compasses are helpful if your design has geometric elements.

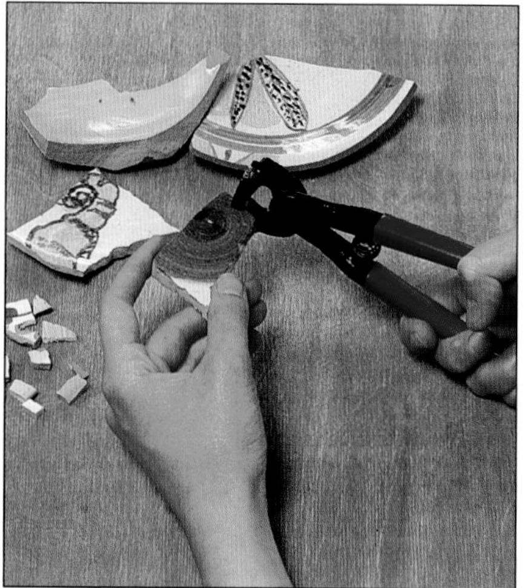

4 Divide the china by colour and pattern and select motifs for the design. Cut the china into small squares using the tile nippers. Use smooth-edged pieces to edge the panel, pressing the pieces into tile adhesive. Use small, regular tesserae to tile the structural lines.

5 Raise small areas of the mosaic by setting the tesserae on a larger mound of adhesive. Fill in the pattern between the structural lines. Leave to dry for about 24 hours.

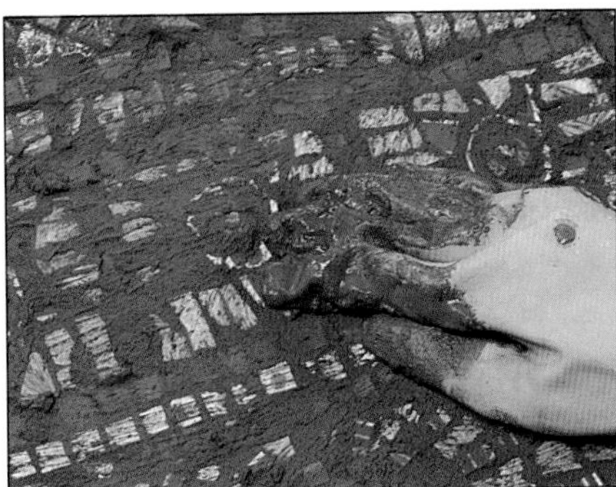

6 Mix powdered grout with water and add cement dye to achieve the colour you want. Wearing rubber gloves, spread the grout over the surface using a squeegee or a flexible (putty) knife and rub into the gaps with your fingers. Allow to dry for a few minutes, then scrub off any excess using a stiff nailbrush. Leave to dry for 24 hours, then polish the mosaic with a soft cloth.

■ ABOVE

This beautiful three-dimensional panel is full of interest, as it is assembled from pieces of patterned china to make a rich pattern of its own.

Stone Effect Wall Mask

It is hard to believe that this wonderful stone-effect wall mask, evocative of medieval times, was created from terracotta-coloured plastic, bought from a garden centre at an affordable price. The slightly pitted quality of the plastic makes it very suitable for painting, which successfully disguises the original material. Once the mask is in position on the wall, nobody would suspect that it is not made from natural stone.

■ RIGHT
A framing of plants around the mask encourages the illusion that it is an old stone feature of the garden wall.

1 Rub down the wall mask with sandpaper and paint it with acrylic primer. Let it dry for 1–2 hours. Paint with a coat of stone-coloured emulsion (latex) and leave to dry for 2 hours.

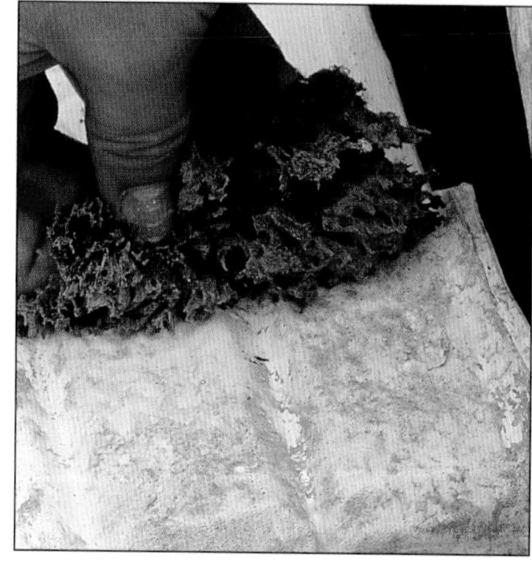

2 Tint some acrylic scumble glaze with a little raw umber and thin with a little water. Sponge on to the mask. Allow to dry for 1–2 hours.

Tools and Materials

- plastic wall mask
- medium-grade sandpaper
- acrylic primer
- paintbrushes
- emulsion (latex) paint in stone
- acrylic scumble glaze
- artist's acrylic paints in raw umber, white, yellow ochre and burnt umber
- natural sponge
- matt polyurethane exterior varnish

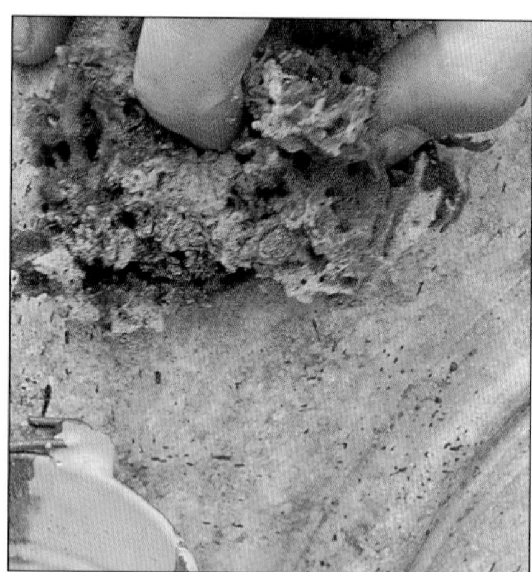

3 Tint some white acrylic paint with a little yellow ochre. Add some scumble glaze and sponge on. Allow to dry for 1–2 hours.

4 Tint some more white acrylic paint with burnt umber and thin as before. Load a large artist's paintbrush and spatter the paint on to the mask with flicking movements. Leave to dry, then varnish the mask.

Water Features

Of all the fixtures in the garden, water features are surely the most entrancing. The gentle sound of water trickling, pattering or gurgling has a wonderfully relaxing effect and the glinting, reflective surface brings a new dimension to the garden. It doesn't have to be a grand affair – there is room for a water feature in even the smallest back yard.

Water features can range from a miniature fountain bubbling up through pebbles to a naturalistic pond that would be at home in a cottage-style garden. In between are formal ponds that can be round, rectangular or even T-shaped. At its simplest, a water feature could be just a garden hosepipe, gently splashing water on to a pile of pebbles below.

Whatever your choice, the water should be kept moving to prevent it from becoming stagnant, and that means organizing a small pump to circulate the water. Submersible pumps can be placed at the bottom of ponds, and some wall masks come already fitted with a pump. You will obviously need to have an electricity supply available where you want to site your water feature, so it is best to plan this before the garden is landscaped or paving laid. An outdoor supply should always be installed by a qualified electrician.

Apart from the electrical side, putting in a pond is not beyond anyone who is handy around the house, especially if you use a pond liner. There is a choice of pre-moulded fibreglass linings and the more easily disguised flexible butyl rubber or plastic sheeting. Once the liner is in place, you can cover its edges with rocks, pebbles and clever planting.

It is best not to site the pond beneath overhanging branches, as autumn leaves will fall directly into it, contaminating the pond as they decay.

■ LEFT
A formal geometric pond with oriental overtones makes a stunning focal point in a small town garden.

If you have small children, opt for a water feature that does not require any depth of water (such as a fountain that drains through pebbles) as a toddler can drown in just a few centimetres of water. Even if you want to plan a larger pool in the long term, you could fill it with pebbles to begin with, letting a fountain splash over these until the children are older and the pebbles can be removed.

■ ABOVE
A delightful miniature pond, filled with water-lilies, has been made in a large glazed earthenware pot, which can be "planted" in the border.

■ ABOVE
This water feature has been planned as part of the garden architecture and is set within a brick-built arch on the wall, which has then been lined with flint pebbles for a rich texture.

■ ABOVE
A well-positioned pond gives visual impact to a garden, and can be used to add interest to a large expanse of lawn.

■ RIGHT
An enchanting little pond, complete with fountain and cherub, mimics designs on a much grander scale.

Shell Fountain

Shells are a natural choice for a water feature. Here, water pours from the mouth of a large snail shell into a series of scallop shells to create a waterfall that flows into a large earthenware pot. The water is pumped back up and through a hole in the back of the snail shell, and the fountain is completed with an edging of more shells and some leafy plants.

■ OPPOSITE
Position this small fountain in a shady corner of the garden to add its gentle sound to a restful spot out of the hot summer sun.

Tools and Materials

- damp cloth
- galvanized metal tub
- red oxide paint
- paintbrush
- 5 scallop shells
- old, broken hip tile or similar
- marker pen
- drill
- 5 wall plugs
- hacksaw
- file
- 5 brass screws
- screwdriver
- large snail shell
- round file
- small pump
- fine garden wire
- pliers
- butyl rubber pond liner
- glazed ceramic pot
- sponge
- stones
- scissors
- assorted shells
- potted plants
- fine gravel
- bolt
- small wall planter

1 Rub the galvanized metal tub with a damp cloth to ensure it is free of dirt and grease. Paint the galvanized tub with red oxide paint and leave to dry.

2 Arrange the scallop shells inside the hip tile, with the largest shell at the base, and mark their positions. Drill a hole at each mark, inside the tile, and an extra hole next to the top hole. Fit all except the last hole with wall plugs.

3 Using a hacksaw, trim the bases of the shells to a right-angle to fit inside the tile. File the edges as necessary.

4 Drill a hole in the base of each shell and screw into the hip tile, arranging the shells in order of size.

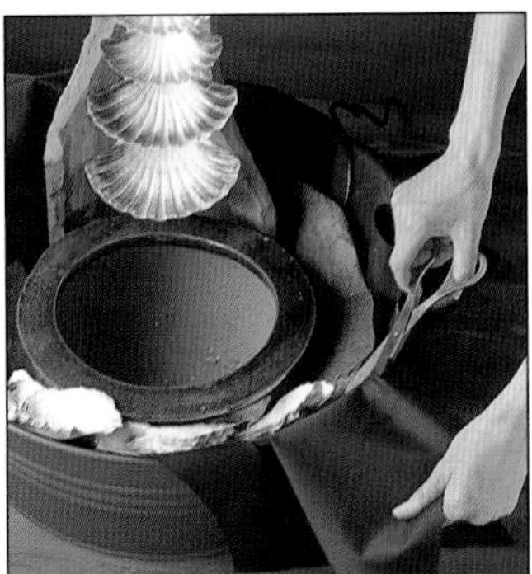

5 Drill a hole in the back of the large snail shell, taking care not to drill through the rest of the shell. Enlarge the hole with a round file and insert the hose.

6 Attach the snail shell to the top of the hip tile using garden wire. Loop the wire under the top scallop shell and twist the ends together.

7 Line the galvanized tub with a butyl rubber liner and place a ceramic pot inside with the shell fountain behind it. Place the pump out of sight behind the tile, surrounding it with sponge to support it. Fill the tub with stones.

8 Trim the excess pond liner and arrange shells and potted plants around the top of the tub. Sprinkle some fine gravel over the shells. Bolt a small wall planter on to the hip tile through the extra hole drilled at the top, then add a trailing plant.

Decorative Storage

Gardeners accumulate an extraordinary amount of practical paraphernalia. Tools, pots and planters, potting compost, raffia, string, seeds and baskets are but a few of the bulky and space-consuming examples. For tools and equipment, a garden shed is the classic solution, though in a smaller garden you may be restricted to a mini-shed or tool store, which might be as small as 30cm/12in deep, tucked into a corner. Sheds can become an attractive part of the garden architecture if painted and decorated sympathetically.

■ OPPOSITE
While storage space is always necessary in the garden, it is often uninspiring to look at. Here, a tall-growing sunflower and splashes of plant colour, teamed with a birdhouse and bird-feeding table, have helped to make a charming feature of this old garden shed.

Putting your goods on show is one option for decorative storage. Garden pots can be very fetching and, displayed on all-weather shelves, can become part of the garden design. This is an excellent solution for very small gardens and patios, all of which still need space for the practicals. Instead of buying ready-made garden shelving, you could build your own from timber and decorate it with exterior-quality paint. Metal shelves old and new can be given a new life using car spray paint or specially manufactured metal paint, which can even be sprayed straight over rust. All shelves should be fixed firmly to the garden wall – avoid using the house wall for this as it could lead to damp problems indoors. Once fitted, use the shelves for displays, to store tools, or for bringing on young seedlings, which can look delightful potted up in ranks of terracotta.

For less attractive, but still essential, garden features such as rubbish bins (trash cans) and fuel stores, disguise is by far the best policy. One of the simplest solutions is to paint the object to blend it in with the surrounding garden. Alternatively, the object can be screened from view using large plants, abundant foliage or trellis. Where space is at a premium, a trellis screen furnished with climbing plants is a more compact option than large shrubs.

■ LEFT
Old French baker's shelves make a practical and attractive garden nursery for growing seedlings.

■ BELOW

Old clay pots make a decorative corner display on a blue-painted plant stand.

■ ABOVE

A thoughtful attempt to beautify an old garden shed has also found a solution to a common gardening problem. Gardening equipment attached to the outside of the shed looks very decorative and helps the gardener find what he is looking for when he needs it.

■ ABOVE

Shelving can be used for purely decorative purposes outside as well as in. Here, a few well-chosen pebbles, arranged on a blue-painted shelf mounted on corbels, make a pretty detail in the garden.

■ ABOVE

Garden sheds typically store a mixed assortment of items, but far from being unsightly, these jumbled collections have an attractive earthy appeal.

Decorative Garden Furniture

To make your garden a space you can really live in, it must be furnished: choose comfortable-looking pieces that will tempt you to go outside, kick off your shoes and relax, soaking up the sun or cooling off in the shade.

A vast range of garden furniture is available but you can narrow down your options by deciding whether you want your furnishings to be permanent fixtures or moveable feasts. Lightweight garden furniture is inexpensive but often lacks glamour, and makes a good candidate for customized paint treatments, or embellishments with cushions and cloths. Wooden or stone furniture is expensive to buy, but it makes a long-term investment that will add an architectural dimension to your garden all through the year.

Garden furniture performs a practical function, but it is also decorative and can be as quirky as you like. For a really exotic touch, fix a hammock between a couple of trees, or drape an awning around a group of chairs and while away some happy hours in elegant relaxation.

■ ABOVE
The relaxed elegance of this classic garden seat makes it a feature in itself.

■ OPPOSITE
A simple slatted chair is easily customized with a few coats of paint.

Choosing Garden Furniture

There is an enormous range of furniture available for the garden, from folding metal or canvas chairs, which can be stored in a shed and just brought out when they are needed, to whole suites of hardwood dining furniture. While you may not want your garden to be cluttered with enough chairs to seat a crowd all the time, a few carefully placed permanent fixtures, such as a weatherproof hardwood bench, a metal table and a few chairs on the patio or an inviting wooden bench under an arbour, all play an important role in the garden's structure and make it look especially welcoming and lived-in.

If you fancy a quick coffee break in a brief burst of spring sunshine, you won't want to spend time searching in the shed for a chair to sit on, and a plain wooden bench that lives all year long in the garden is just the place for a breather during a heavy digging session on a cold winter's day.

For furniture that is to be left outside all year, choose durable materials such as painted metal or hardwood (from sustainable sources). Softer woods should be hardened and will need treating with preservative, which will need renewing at least once a year for it to remain effective. Plastic furniture needs little maintenance except for washing, but it has a limited life outdoors and will eventually become brittle and easily breakable.

Other highly decorative materials that are also comfortable include wicker and Lloyd loom, but these are not weatherproof and will need to be stored in a garden shed, garage or conservatory when not in use.

■ RIGHT
This unique piece of furniture, half-chair and half-sculpture, is made from driftwood and fencing stakes, and is perfect for an outdoor setting.

■ RIGHT
Wicker furniture is comfortable, especially if cushions are added to fit the seats. It will look good in any garden setting. Used outside in summer, it will weather to a subtle natural shade, or it can be painted for a brighter look.

■ BELOW
Traditional slatted folding chairs look pretty in the garden and make perfect seating for an al fresco dinner party.

■ RIGHT
Metal furniture is robust enough to need very little maintenance, and can be kept outside throughout the year.

Garden Chairs

Furnishing the garden gives you somewhere to sit and relax and, at the same time, adds to the architectural element of the garden. Some furniture – a traditional stone seat, for example – is designed to be an almost permanent part of the garden; certainly stone seats are not moved with regularity.

Architecturally, permanent seating provides another step up visually, with its legs equal to balustrades. While such wonderful garden fixtures aren't really within most people's budgets, a similar role is played by old wooden garden benches, which, as they weather to a soft green-tinged grey, take on a permanent air as part of the garden architecture.

Single benches exude a peaceful air, probably because they are not conducive to conversation but are more for sitting and contemplating. Love seats, designed in an S-shape, are far more sociable since the occupants sit facing each other. Groups of chairs around an outdoor table represent social times in the garden, whether you are simply eating outside with the family, taking tea with a friend or having an evening party.

In high summer, there is nothing more enjoyable than lounging around in the garden, and this is when the softer, more reclining types of chair, including canvas deck-chairs and directors' chairs, come into their own. The lounger is the lotus-eater's dream – more day-bed than chair. Wood-slatted steamer chairs were the original loungers, designed for use on long voyages. Their modern equivalents – in wood, metal, or plastic – are fitted with upholstered cushions. Hammocks are another kind of day-bed, and, gently swaying between a pair of trees, they would challenge anyone to stay awake.

■ BELOW
This witty, plastic-covered Louis XIV chair offers indoor elegance outside.

■ ABOVE
Softly weathered wooden furniture fits easily into almost any garden setting.

■ LEFT
This modern wrought-iron furniture is inspired by the French styles of the last century, the elegant lightweight lines of which are now enjoying a revival.

■ RIGHT
Furniture makes its own contribution to the look of the garden and, if it's not being used to sit on, it can make an ideal backdrop for decorative garden "pieces".

■ BELOW
Elaborate cast-iron furniture became a favourite in Victorian times, and its popularity has not waned. Its price, however, means you are more likely to see it as a feature in public parks than in private gardens.

■ RIGHT
An old Lloyd loom chair was given a fresh look a few years ago with two shades of blue spray car paint. Even though the finish is now rather worn, the chair exudes a comfortable, cottage-garden feel.

String and Driftwood Chair

You can transform an ordinary chair into something quite special by binding it with jute or garden string and attaching pieces of driftwood collected from the beach. Here, awkward joins are decorated with pieces of flotsam and jetsam, and two "horns" give a dramatic shape to the chair back. Making or changing furniture can be just a matter of using what is at hand. String is hardwearing, cheap, and gives this chair a tactile quality. Other decorative materials include bark, twigs or shells, collected on walks or at the beach.

1 Cut jute or string into manageable lengths and roll these into small balls. Glue the end of a string ball firmly to the top of the chair. You will need to do this each time you start a new ball.

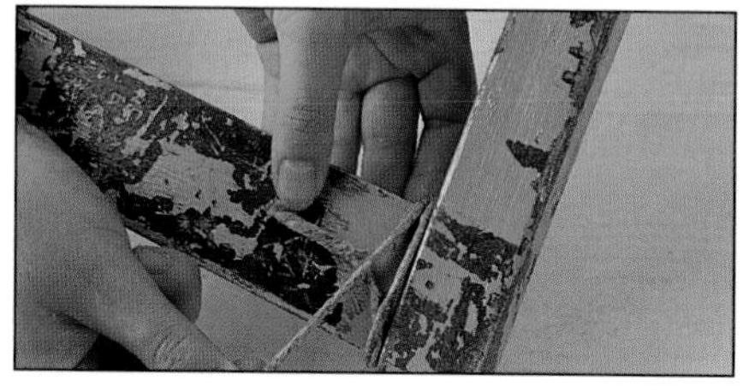

2 Run a thin line of glue along the back of the chair to secure the string. Starting at one end, pull the string taut as you wrap it around the chair.

Tools and Materials

- ball of jute or garden string
- scissors
- glue gun
- chair
- pieces of driftwood

3 Make two criss-cross patterns along the middle of the chair back to decorate. Hold them in place with glue.

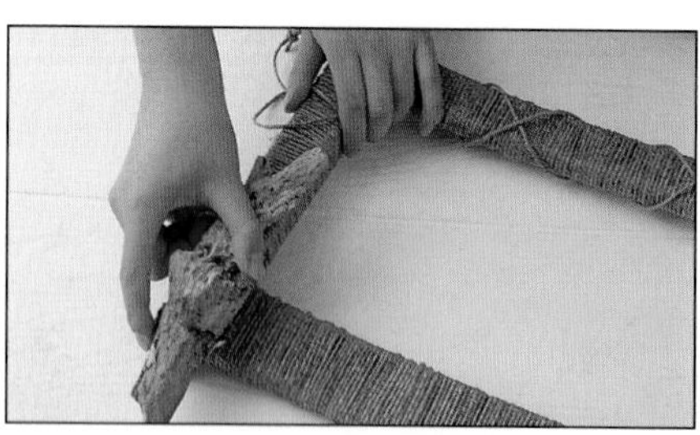

4 Glue the driftwood to the top of the chair and secure with string. To finish off, knot and bind the string underneath.

■ RIGHT
Revive an old chair by taking a fresh look at everyday materials.

Sea-weathered Director's Chair

This aging technique instantly transforms furniture from new to old, imbuing the wood with an interesting weathered quality and allowing it to blend perfectly into its outdoor surroundings. Getting away from a pristine paint surface and acquiring an old, worn look makes furniture more comfortable to live with and more relaxing to look at.

Tools and Materials

- director's chair
- scrubbing brush
- bucket
- soapy water
- cloth
- masking tape
- household candle
- emulsion (latex) paint in pale blue and white
- paintbrushes
- sandpaper
- matt acrylic varnish

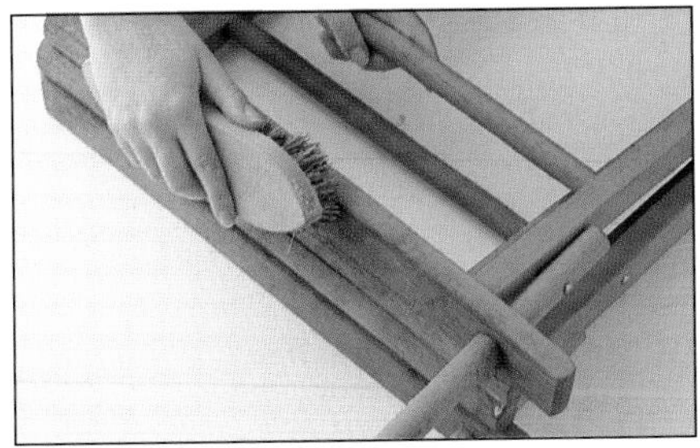

1 Remove the fabric from the chair and scrub the wood with soapy water. Wipe down with a dry cloth. Let dry.

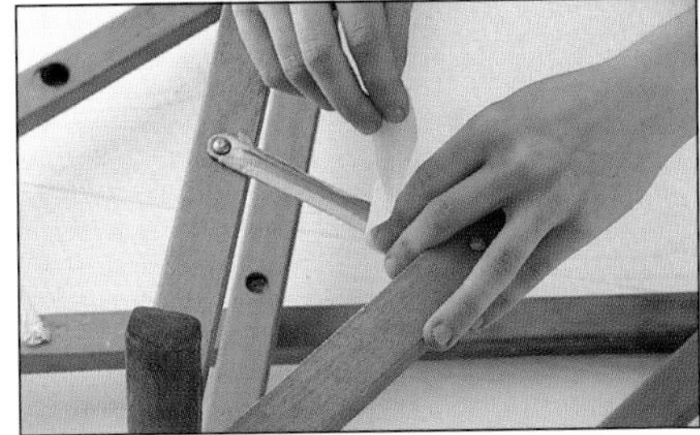

2 Cover all the metal attachments with masking tape. Rub the wood with a candle, concentrating on the areas that would naturally show wear, such as the edges and corners. Dilute the pale blue emulsion (latex) 3:1 with water and paint over the chair frame. Leave to dry.

3 Rub over the paint with sandpaper to reveal the wood beneath, then rub all over with the candle again. Dilute the white emulsion 3:1 with water and paint the chair frame. Leave to dry.

4 Rub with sandpaper to reveal areas of wood and the blue paint. Seal with matt varnish, let dry and replace the fabric.

■ BELOW
Director's chairs are inexpensive, portable and easy to store – turn yours into furniture that's worth a second look with a simple distressing technique.

Crazy Paving Chair

This old chair, found rejected and battered in a junk shop, has been transformed into an exciting, unusual piece of furniture. It is covered in tesserae cut from a selection of china, and it's important to be aware that a large three-dimensional object like this requires a deceptively large amount of mosaic to cover it, so you would be lucky to find enough china of a single pattern. Here, the problem has been solved by using slightly different designs to cover different sections of the chair.

■ OPPOSITE
Applying mosaic to an old chair turns it into a beguilingly original piece of furniture and a focal point in the garden.

Tools and Materials

- chair
- 2cm/¾in plywood
- paint stripper
- coarse-grade sandpaper
- paintbrush
- PVA (white) glue
- wood glue
- cement-based tile adhesive
- flexible (putty) knife
- pencil or chalk
- large selection of old china
- tile nippers
- powdered tile grout
- rubber gloves
- stiff nailbrush
- soft cloth

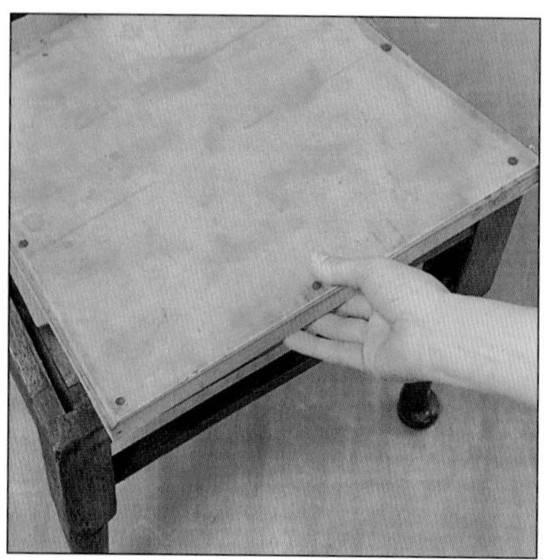

1 If the chair has a padded seat, remove it and replace it with a piece of plywood cut to fit the frame. Strip off any paint or varnish and rub down with coarse sandpaper. Paint the whole chair with diluted PVA (white) glue.

2 When the surface is dry, stick the seat in place with wood glue and fill any gaps with cement-based tile adhesive.

3 Draw a design or motifs on any large flat surfaces of the chair, using simple shapes that are easy to follow such as this flower.

4 Select china with colours and patterns to suit your design. Using tile nippers, cut the china into the appropriate sizes and shapes.

5 Spread cement-based tile adhesive within the areas of your design and press the china tesserae firmly into it.

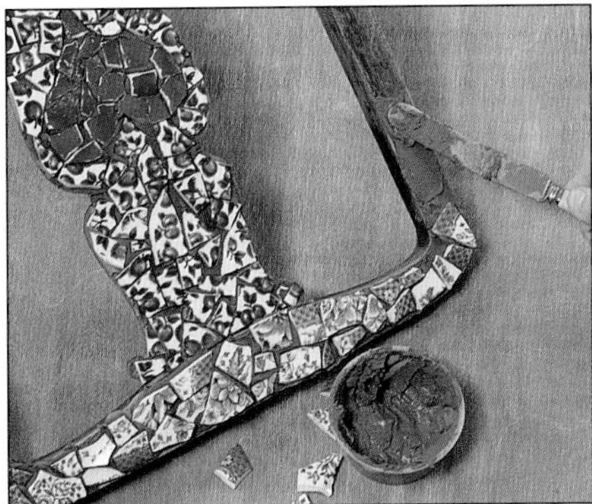

6 Working on small areas at a time, tile the rest of the chair. Where one section of wood meets another, change the pattern of the china. Cut the china into thin slivers to tile the edges of the chair. Leave to dry for at least 24 hours.

7 Using a flexible (putty) knife, grout the mosaic with the tile adhesive. Wearing rubber gloves, rub the grout over the flat surfaces, cleaning off the excess as you work. Leave to dry.

8 When the grout is completely dry, sand off any excess cement with sandpaper or a stiff nailbrush. Polish with a soft cloth to buff up the china.

A Lick of Paint

Co-ordinating furniture with its surroundings helps to give the garden a harmonious ambience. By painting old furniture, you can also keep the costs down, as you can pick up bargain pieces from junk shops or simply rejuvenate old kitchen chairs that are due for replacement. And you can be sure of perfect toning as paints come in literally hundreds of shades. These chairs were most unprepossessing when they were picked up: the slatted ones were peeling and the Tyrolean-style chair was finished with a tired old varnish.

■ OPPOSITE
Clashing Caribbean colours of pink and tangerine make for a lively look in a brightly coloured garden.

■ BELOW
Taupe and white make an elegant combination for a chair with Italian-style flair. It is an ideal finish for a garden that features a lot of natural wood tones.

■ ABOVE
This Tyrolean-style chair is given a bright, modern finish to team with the painted shed wall behind. It also co-ordinates well with silver-grey foliage and lipstick-pink flowers.

Weathering and Distressing

When looking around antique shops that specialize in old garden furniture, it can be quite shocking to see the prices charged for these items. Simple folding chairs, once used in their thousands in public parks, are now desirable objects with their faded paintwork and weathered wood, and they fetch premium prices. A far less expensive alternative is to buy new hardwood folding chairs and do a bit of instant weathering yourself. Four chairs transformed in this way will cost about the same as one antique chair. The weathered effect is achieved by sanding down the surface, rubbing with wax, then painting and rubbing down again. When the chair is left out in the garden, nature will continue the weathering process, and within a season you will have your own set of heirlooms.

Tools and Materials

- folding wooden garden chair
- medium-grade sandpaper
- household candle
- white emulsion (latex) paint
- paintbrush
- wire (steel) wool

1 Sandpaper the surface of the chair to make a key so that the paint adheres. Rub over the surface randomly with the candle, applying the wax thickly on the edges and corners.

2 Paint the chair with several coats of white emulsion (latex) paint, using random strokes, and leave to dry.

3 When the paint is dry, rub the paintwork with wire (steel) wool to remove the paint from the waxed areas, so that the wood is showing. Wipe the chair with a damp cloth to clean away the dust, and leave to dry.

■ OPPOSITE
Charmingly weathered and worn, this wooden chair looks as if it has been standing in the garden for years.

Decorative Deck-chairs

There is little in the way of garden furniture to beat the practicality of deck-chairs. They have a traditional, comfortable look, and with the occasional new cover they will last more than a lifetime. You can buy striped deck-chair canvas and simply nail it on, but why not go a step or two further and add some pattern to a plain canvas? It really is not difficult, even if you have never considered yourself to be an expert with a paintbrush. One of these designs was made with a ready-cut stencil and the other with tracings of traditional bird motifs from copyright-free or clip art collections.

"Indian Birds" Design

1. Wash, rinse, dry and iron the canvas to remove any dressing. Remove the deck-chair canvas and paint the frame with woodstain.

2. Trace a selection of traditional bird motifs (published in out-of-copyright collections). Using a soft pencil, scribble on the back. Place the tracing in position on the canvas and draw over the lines with a hard pencil to transfer the design.

3. Colour in the birds using soft fabric pens. For the border, measure 2cm/¾in from the edge of the canvas and place masking tape along the length. Draw a wavy line down the edge, then, with a contrasting pen, fill in the edges. Repeat for the inner borders, placing a strip of masking tape either side.

4. When the ink is dry, set it by covering with a white cloth and pressing with a hot iron, covering each part for at least 2 minutes. Use upholstery tacks or panel pins (tacks) to fix the canvas securely to the top and bottom of the chair.

"Stencil Rug" Design

1. Prepare the canvas and the deck-chair as for the "Indian Birds" design. Plan the design.

2. Work out the areas of the design before you start. Starting with the borders, fix the stencil in position using masking tape. Load the stencil brush with paint and remove any excess on newspaper. Apply this colour through the stencil. Repeat until all areas of the colour have been painted. Let dry.

3. Reposition the stencil over the original colour and apply a fresh colour. Repeat until the design is complete. Set the paint and attach the canvas to the chair as for the "Indian Birds" design.

Tools and Materials

For the "Indian Birds" design:

- deck-chair
- 1.5m/5ft length deck-chair canvas
- exterior woodstain
- paintbrush
- soft and hard pencils
- tracing paper
- bird motifs from copyright-free or clip art collections
- soft fabric pens in red, green, purple, yellow and blue
- ruler
- masking tape
- white cloth
- iron
- dome-headed upholstery tacks or panel pins (tacks)

For the "Stencilled Rug" design:

- deck-chair
- 1.5m/5ft length deck-chair canvas
- exterior woodstain
- paintbrush
- ready-cut stencil
- masking tape
- stencil brush
- stencil paints in red, ochre, olive and aqua
- newspaper
- white cloth
- iron
- dome-headed upholstery tacks

■ LEFT
Trace traditional motifs in a repeating design for the border of the canvas.

■ ABOVE
There's no need to stick to traditional deck-chair stripes. Decorate plain canvas to your own designs to make original, stylish garden chairs.

■ ABOVE
Ready-cut stencils are available in hundreds of designs and can be combined however you like to make abstract patterns.

■ ABOVE
Woodstain, a length of vivid canvas and some soft fabric pens are all you need to revitalize an old deck-chair.

■ ABOVE
Stencilling is a very quick way to create an individual design for a deck-chair.

Garden Tables

A table is at the heart of a whole way of life in the garden. As long as the weather holds, it can take the place of the dining table, the kitchen worktop and the writing desk indoors. Once you have a table in the garden you will use every excuse to use it for breakfast, lunch and dinner – a light lunch, the children's tea, or an intimate supper. Meals outside, when the weather is balmy and the evenings long, are invariably happier and more relaxed, with the air of a picnic.

Choose a table that is substantial but not too huge, solid and not wobbly, and weatherproof so that it becomes a more or less permanent fixture in the garden. You can make your eating area into a garden room, defining the space with a screen of trellis, flower borders, a sheltering arbour, or banks of plants in containers. A pergola overhead will give dappled shade and a sense of privacy.

■ ABOVE
Paint a simple metal tabletop with a shell design then add a wash over the top to give it a weathered look. Varnish the surface to protect it.

■ LEFT
This design has bold lines and strong contrasts that suit the chunky crazy-paving style of the mosaic. It is worked on a plain round wooden table top, screwed to a metal base.

■ RIGHT
Mosaic makes an enduring surface for a garden table, and adds a rich colour accent to the garden as a whole.

■ BELOW
However battered by time and weather, delicate old wrought-iron furniture retains its air of refinement and goes on looking pretty in the garden.

Wooden Garden Table

This sturdy table is ideal for the garden because the wood is already weathered and further aging will make it look even better. You can leave it out all year round without worrying about it, though an occasional coat of clear wood preservative would lengthen its life. The table top here measures 74 x 75cm/ 29 x 30in, but you can adapt the design to the size you require.

■ OPPOSITE
This rustic "occasional" table will happily live in the garden through all weathers, and would be perfect near a favourite garden seat as a place to put down a cup or glass, a book or a shady hat.

Tools and Materials

- 5 weathered planks, 74 x 15cm/ 29 x 6in
- tape measure
- saw
- 1m/39in weathered batten, 5 x 1cm/2 x ½in
- electric drill
- screwdriver
- 4cm/1½in screws
- 4 wooden poles and thick sticks
- hammer
- 7.5cm/3in and 4cm/1½in nails
- pencil
- string

1 Lay the planks side by side. Cut two 48cm/19in lengths of batten, drill holes then screw across the planks about 7.5cm/3in in from either end to make the table top.

2 Saw the four poles into 90cm/36in lengths, for the legs. Cut four sticks 43cm/17in long.

3 Nail a stick a quarter of the way in from each end of each pair of legs, to make two side frames.

4 Lay the table top upside down. Centre the side frames on the battens and draw around the top of each leg.

5 Drill a pilot hole through the centre of each circle.

6 With the table top supported on one side frame, nail through into the legs. Repeat for the other side frame.

7 Cut a thick stick 62cm/25in long. Hold in place and nail it across the two side frames at the back of the table.

8 To stabilize the table, make a cross frame. Cut two lengths of stick 90cm/3ft long and nail each to a front leg and the opposite back leg. Bind with string where the sticks cross in the centre.

Mosaic Garden Table

This striking mosaic table top is made from pieces of broken china pots and chipped decorative tiles, and with clever colour co-ordination and a simple, clear design, it makes the most attractive, weatherproof garden furniture. Although it is resilient to damp, bringing it inside over the winter will give it a longer life.

■ OPPOSITE
Mount the mosaic table top on metal or wooden legs, or simply screw it to an old circular table that is past its prime.

Tools and Materials

- 2.5cm/1in plywood at least 120cm/4ft square
- string
- drawing pin
- pencil
- jigsaw
- wood primer
- paintbrush
- tile nippers
- large selection of broken china
- tile adhesive
- tile grout
- grout colour
- rubber gloves
- washing-up brush
- cloth

PREPARATION
To mark out the circle, tie a piece of string to a drawing pin at one end and push the pin into the centre of the plywood. Tie a pencil to the other end of the string to give you a radius of 60cm/2ft. Draw the circle and cut out using a jigsaw.

1 Draw the design on the plywood circle, adjusting the length of string to draw concentric circles.

2 Prime the table with wood primer and leave to dry.

3 Use tile nippers to cut the broken china into pieces to fit the design and try it out on the table top. Use motifs on the china as focal points in the design.

4 When the design is complete, work across the table top a section at a time, "buttering" each piece of china with adhesive and sticking it in position.

5 Mix the grout with the colour and, wearing rubber gloves, use your fingers to work the grout in between the mosaic pieces. Complete the grouting by scrubbing over the surface using a washing-up brush. Clean off any excess.

Garden Console

This console table was designed for a conventional indoor life, but has been given an outdoor paint treatment for a witty touch in the garden. It makes a useful extra surface for drinks or serving dishes when you are entertaining outside.

Tools and Materials

- console table
- medium-grade sandpaper
- white acrylic wood primer
- medium and fine paintbrushes
- masonry paint
- artist's acrylic paints in terracotta and pink
- fine-textured masonry paint
- acrylic scumble glaze
- cloth
- pencil
- stencil cardboard
- craft knife
- stencil brush
- polyurethane varnish
- varnish brush

1 Prepare the table by sanding all the surfaces thoroughly. Prime with white acrylic wood primer and allow to dry. Tint some masonry paint with terracotta acrylic and use as a base coat. Allow to dry for 4–6 hours.

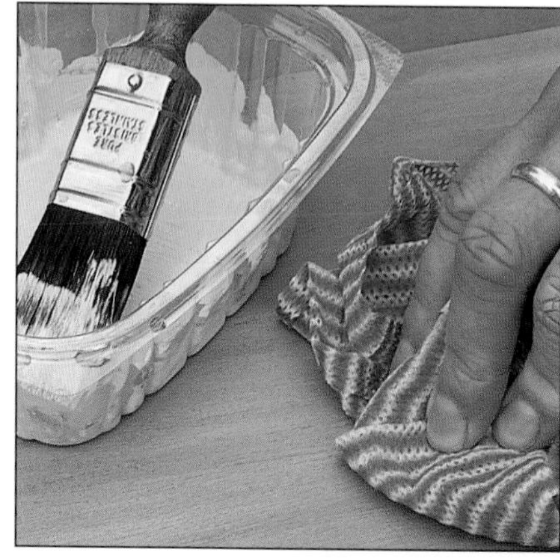

2 Tint some fine-textured masonry paint with pink acrylic, add scumble glaze and thin with water to the consistency of double cream. Paint on and rub off with a cloth in the direction of the grain. Allow to dry.

3 Draw a leaf shape on a piece of stencil cardboard and cut out. Use terracotta paint to stencil a leaf on each corner of the table. Allow to dry, then varnish.

■ OPPOSITE
When the console table is not being used, you can have fun accessorizing it as if it were standing in a room indoors.

■ RIGHT
The essence of outdoor style is its simplicity. This garden store cupboard was built from nailed together pieces of driftwood.

Awnings and Umbrellas

Living outside sometimes requires shelter from the wind, or shade from a blistering sun. On a breezy day, a windbreak of some kind will enable you to sit outside even in early spring or autumn. A capacious umbrella or parasol, on the other hand, will allow you to eat outside or simply relax in its shade even in the middle of the day in high summer; and if you want to bask in the sunshine at lunchtime, the food on the table will always benefit from being kept in the shade, out of reach from the glaring sun.

If you have rejected the idea of building a pergola over your patio because it casts too much shade in winter, a more adaptable alternative could be a canvas awning. This will give instant shade on a hot day – and also keep the sun off the house windows, helping to cool the interior – but can be rolled back to the wall on cooler days when you would prefer to sit in the sun.

If you prefer to move in line with the sun, a large portable umbrella with a weighted base can be put up anywhere in the garden.

■ ABOVE
Four chairs, a table and an umbrella instantly make a pleasantly informal seating arrangement – a portable arbour from which to enjoy the garden.

■ OPPOSITE
A dead tree provided the inspiration for this elaborate sheltered seating area. The natural awning was constructed from the pruned branches of the tree, while a dovecote on the top means that those sitting beneath the shelter can enjoy the sounds of the visiting birds.

■ ABOVE LEFT
Late summer tasks, such as topping and tailing fruit, become pleasurable pastimes under an awning. Original Edwardian awnings like this consist of a lightweight metal frame that is easily erected before slipping the canvas cover over the top.

Plants in Pots: The Soft Furnishings

Like vases of fresh flowers indoors, plants in containers provide strong accents of shape and colour in the garden, softening the lines of garden structures. They are prima donnas, flaunting their vivid colours while they are in their full glory, then bowing out to be replaced by the next star turn.

Decorative planting is one of the more pleasurable aspects of having an outdoor space. More than anything else, the choice of plants – and the containers they're planted in – will affect the mood of the garden and the finished look. Group containers by colour or create cameo gardens along a theme. Use an eclectic mix of containers or trim and shape shrubs and plants for a witty effect. Window boxes and hanging baskets will add special plant interest, especially if potted with more unusual plant options such as wild strawberries or fresh herbs.

■ ABOVE
Group plants together for a mass of colour and a vibrant display.

■ OPPOSITE
There are no rules when it comes to arranging potted plants, and a witty and original choice of container will add something special.

DECORATIVE PLANTINGS

Once the basic framework of the garden is in place, the fun can start. Indoors, once you had painted the walls and laid the floors, you would be thinking of comfortable furniture, curtains and carpets. Outside, it is the planting that provides the soft furnishing. Without it, the garden would look very rigid and uninviting. Add a few plants, and immediately it takes on a much more comfortable feel. This is the part of gardening that is the most absorbing, even if you start off with no horticultural knowledge. A trip to the garden centre to browse among the seasonal plants becomes a treat.

Putting together the colours and textures to compose beautiful borders is one of the more pleasurable aspects of gardening, and is where your own creativity comes in. But soft furnishing in the context of the decorated garden is not just about borders. Decorative planting is about climbers that clamber curtain-like over arches and soften the outlines of vistas, and the hanging baskets that decorate walls. It is about the low-growing plants that create carpets of colour over what may previously have been uninspiring bare ground, and the plants that grow around and through established trees and shrubs, softening and beautifying their outlines. It is, finally, about feature planting in containers, positioned at focal points in the garden to create interest and impact.

■ OPPOSITE
A floral arbour makes a rich decorative frame for a piece of statuary, creating a theatrical effect. The roses, foxgloves and clematis make perfect stage curtains for this thoughtful stone "player".

■ BELOW
Trellis makes a permanent light screen across part of the garden, curtained in summer by the glossy green foliage and vivid flowers of a climbing rose.

■ ABOVE
The face of a cherub, in reflective mood, peers through the ivy, adding a charming touch to the eaves of a garden shed.

■ LEFT
Statuesque Greek pithoi are used here for architectural interest, rather than for planting. However, they have been softened and beautifully set off by stately euphorbias in vibrant shades of lime green.

Colour Theme Plantings

Create impact in the garden by colour-theming seasonal planting to match the colours of your garden fixtures. This works best with plants in containers, as pots and planters can be chosen or painted to tone with the walls and fences, then planted with flowers in complementary colours. Once the blooms are over, they can be replaced by new plantings for the next season. You don't have to match the colours: using complementary or contrasting colours may be just as effective. In this way, the garden looks fresh and bright all year round, and you have several changes of scene as the seasons pass.

■ BELOW
Fences stained in soft, grey-blue greens set off all manner of greenery, including the foliage of this hebe. The pot has been painted in stripes to link the greens with the pink flowers.

■ RIGHT
The green-blue and purple tones of ornamental cabbage look fabulous in an old galvanized bucket set against the green-blue background of a painted wooden garden fence.

■ ABOVE
Blues and greys make a wonderful combination and even the most basic pieces of garden paraphernalia can be put to good decorative use. This old, blue-painted wheelbarrow, set against a blue wall, creates impact, while making an original container for delicate violas.

■ RIGHT
A yellow poppy and yellow violas look stunning planted in golden pots, set against the warm ochre of a brick wall.

Colour Splash Plantings

Just as you can decorate the inside of your home with colourful flower arrangements, so you can embellish the outside. Use pots of flowering plants to provide a colourful splash in a prominent part of the garden, or to decorate the outdoor living area when entertaining. Create an immediate impact by choosing a colour theme and teaming containers and plants in toning shades. Try painting some terracotta pots to match your favourite flowers. You could also make a tablescape for a special occasion, using a variety of containers and seasonal flowering plants in hot clashing colours or in cool shades of blue, purple and white.

■ BELOW

Create a colour splash for summer parties. Here, hot colours vie and clash in a fabulous, vibrant display. Simple enamel tableware and a wire "coffee pot" make witty containers for strawberry plants, pelargoniums, verbenas in magenta and scarlet, pansies and daisy-like, yellow creeping zinnia.

■ ABOVE
White-painted pots planted with lily-of-the-valley and placed on a stone bracket make an elegant springtime feature.

■ ABOVE RIGHT
Auriculas planted in an old stone urn and overhung with berberis make a rich spring planting in shades of burnished copper. The display is reminiscent of an old sepia photograph.

■ RIGHT
The blue-green leaves of pinks and oxalis perfectly complement the rich verdigris patina on this old French copper builder's bucket, creating a striking feature that can be hung in the garden or near the house. It's a brilliant way to bring colour up to eye-level in spring, when most plants in flower are low-growing.

Creating Cameo Gardens

It is delightful to plan cameo gardens within gardens. They can present a surprise in a small corner, embellish a less-than-full area of the garden or even provide a miniature project for children, who love to be responsible for a garden area of their very own.

Cameo gardens exist solely on the basis of a theme, be it herbs or pansies, miniature vegetables or lavender. After you have chosen your theme, you then need to make up a "sampler", providing a different container for each variety of your themed plants. If you are making the containers themselves the theme, choose watering cans, cooking pots and pans, enamelware or terracotta in different shapes and sizes. Another idea is to design a miniature formal garden, perhaps taking inspiration from a classic style. Choose a piece of miniature statuary as a focal point, then clip some young box plants into a low hedge around your tiny beds and fill with dwarf lavender.

■ BELOW
Serried ranks of watering cans in the soft greys of weathered, galvanized metal make a beautiful feature in themselves. Planted up with hostas and violas, they form a highly original cameo garden.

■ ABOVE
Thyme gardens have a history that goes back through centuries. Their appeal stems from their irresistible aroma combined with the almost endless number of varieties, with leaves that range in shape from round to needle-like, in texture from smooth to woolly, in colour from silver to darkest green. The trick is to choose a selection that will create a rich tapestry. Planting them in small pots keeps the garden to a scale in which the miniature dimensions of the leaves and their various textures can be appreciated.

■ ABOVE
The intense colour provided by this grouping of grape hyacinths makes a striking display for early spring.

■ RIGHT
This terracotta garden is focused around tall long-tom pots planted with hostas, ivies and a clematis left loose so that it trails rather than climbs. Old drain covers and edging tiles add rich details to the picture.

Witty Ways with Everyday Plants

Interesting gardens don't have to depend on a horticulturalist's expert knowledge of plants. Even the most ordinary plants can take on an exotic personality if pruned or planted in an original way. Many garden centres now sell ready-trained or standardized shrubs – you can add your own touch with a witty container, pretty underplanting or an attractive way of tying up the plants. There are no restrictions to the look you can create.

Topiary has come back into fashion, but this time it isn't restricted to large, formal gardens. Box and privet grown in pots can be kept to a manageable size and still be clipped into architectural globes and conical shapes, as can any other plant which holds its shape well as it grows.

■ ABOVE
A standardized hydrangea grown in a pot makes an excellent patio plant. It has the appealing appearance of a miniature tree, and you can enjoy its flamboyant blooms without any worry that it might take over the garden.

■ ABOVE
Small-scale topiary can be arranged, as here, in groups or used as boundary markers, down the edges of paths, between beds or to section off different parts of the garden.

■ ABOVE
As a change from allowing roses to scramble up walls or trellis, this one has been trained around a simple obelisk, the diagonally trailing stems adding greatly to its decorative appeal.

■ ABOVE
A potted chilli pepper plant would add a fun touch to any garden.

■ RIGHT
Fruit trees can be included in even the smallest gardens. Here, a decorative, apple is flanked by ballerina crab apples, which grow in a pole-like fashion.

Plants and Containers

The best way to create impact with seasonal flowers is to contain them in pots or some kind of container: that way you can mass colour in the plantings and group or stack the pots together for an even greater show.

Containers look fabulous in any garden – first, because the vessels themselves, however simple, give architectural form; second, because they allow you to put the plants and colour exactly where you want them. You need a little colour higher up? Plant up a plant stand, hanging basket or wall-pot. You need a little extra colour in a flower bed? Fill a pot with vivid flowers and set it down among the greenery. You can even plant up small pots to nestle on top of the soil in larger pots for a rich, stacked effect.

CLAY POTS AND PLANTERS

There is little to beat the earthy beauty of ordinary clay pots. They blend well with their surroundings and complement virtually every type of plant. Make sure they are frostproof if they are to stay

■ OPPOSITE
For a gloriously rich, banked window display, one window box has been fixed to the front edge of the windowsill, while the other sits on the ledge. The planting scheme of petunias and dianthus in pinks and purples creates a greater impact for being colour co-ordinated, and it is complemented by the huge lilac orbs of the alliums in the foreground.

■ BELOW
White violas in old terracotta pots, white-crusted with age, lend an ethereal air to the white-painted windowsill of a much-used conservatory.

outside when temperatures plummet, otherwise you will find the terracotta flaking off at the rim during the winter months.

The appearance of clay pots depends on where they are made. The typical pots of northern European countries are generally very red in hue, but the colour does soften with age as salts naturally form on the surface. You can hasten this look by scrubbing them with garden lime. Just make up a thick paste by adding a little water to the lime, then brush it on with an old washing-up brush. As the water in the lime dries out, the terracotta will acquire a soft, white bloom. Garden lime is excellent as it is not harmful to the garden (in fact, it is used as a fertilizer), and it won't inhibit the natural mould growth that also enhances the patina of age. Pots can also be aged by rubbing them with natural yogurt then leaving them in a damp, shady place to encourage mould growth, but this takes a little longer.

Clay pots from the sunny Mediterranean look very different to those of northern Europe.

Greek pithoi, for example, traditionally used to store grain and oil, come in many elegant shapes and have a wonderful sandy colour. Some are even frostproof.

ORIGINAL IDEAS

Your choice does not have to be restricted to garden pots. Any type of container will work, as long as drainage holes can be drilled in the base. Try using old beer barrel halves, decorative ceramic pots, old chimney pots, buckets, agricultural baskets such as potato pickers, or traditional garden baskets such as wooden trugs. With a little imagination, shopping baskets, birdcages and lanterns can be transformed into hanging baskets, and old olive oil cans in a row can become original window boxes.

■ BELOW

All kinds of things can be used to add height to planting – particularly useful in spring and early summer when plants are still small. Here, three small hanging baskets have been stacked on top of each other for brilliant high-level planting.

■ ABOVE

Ornate Chinese ceramic pots make a delightful decorative feature when planted with toning flowering plants, such as pelargoniums and petunias, and accessorized with complementary Chinese statuary.

■ RIGHT

Even a couple of ordinary terracotta garden pots hanging on the wall make an interesting decorative detail when they are both planted with a froth of white blooms.

■ RIGHT
Charming cast-iron panels are used here to enclose ordinary plastic pots of plants – a lovely idea that allows you to replace your plants when they are past their prime, and helps to make seasonal changes painless.

Ideas for Window Boxes

Window boxes give a delightful finish to the outside of a building, and can be enjoyed just as much from inside, almost bringing the garden into the room. They can be filled to overflowing with exuberant summer bedding plants, but this need not be their only season of interest. Foliage plants such as hebes and ivies will look wonderful throughout the winter, interplanted with winter-flowering pansies, which burst into luminous colours whenever the weather is kind. If you include some spring-flowering bulbs when planting your window boxes in the autumn, you will be able to watch the fresh new shoots emerging at close quarters, heralding spring and the start of a new gardening year.

Like other containers, a window box can be moved out of the limelight once it is past its prime and replaced with another box containing a fresh planting. Match wooden boxes to your plants season by season, ringing the changes with a lick of emulsion (latex) paint in a colour chosen to complement the plants for maximum impact.

■ BELOW
The soft shapes of violas and petunias perfectly complement this stencilled wooden window box. The scent of the flowers will drift magically indoors when the windows are open.

■ RIGHT
A window box filled with herbs and placed on the kitchen windowsill is both pretty and useful. This arrangement is planted in an old fruit box, colour-washed to tone with the herbs. Borage has been included: its flowers will provide interest later in the season.

■ RIGHT
Create a fragrant herbal window box to sit outside the kitchen window, ready to use when needed. This one has been planted up with golden sage, chamomile, marjoram and wild strawberry in an old agricultural basket. Yellow bidens have been included for extra colour.

Seashore Window Box

As most window boxes are flat-fronted, they are easier to decorate than round pots. Here, the beautiful dark lustre of mussel shells left over from the dinner table lends impact to a co-ordinated planting of lavender and violas. Experiment with different shapes, using some of the shells face up and the others face down for a more varied effect.

Tools and Materials

- mussel shells
- small terracotta window box
- glue gun
- crocks or pebbles
- compost (soil mix)
- trowel
- water-retaining granules
- slow-release fertilizer granules
- 2 lavender plants
- tray of violas
- watering can

1 Arrange the mussel shells on the sides of the window box. When you are satisfied with your design, fix the shells in position using a glue gun. Leave until the glue has dried.

2 Place a layer of crocks or pebbles over the drainage holes inside the window box.

3 Partly fill the box with compost (soil mix), adding water-retaining and fertilizer granules as you go.

4 Plant the lavender at the back of the box. Press extra compost in front of the lavender until it is the right height for the violas. Plant the violas.

5 Top up with compost, firming it gently around the plants, and water generously.

■ OPPOSITE
The soft petals and subtle colour gradations of the violas make them the perfect match for the pearly interiors of the shells.

Ideas for Hanging Baskets

When you want colour high up in the garden, whether it is to provide a focal point, frame a view or soften the hard lines of a wall or a building, the easiest way is to plant up a container and hang it up. Ready-made hanging baskets are designed so that as the flowers grow they cascade through the sides and spill over the edge in a joyous show of colour, covering the whole basket.

Unlike stand-alone containers, hanging baskets will need lining inside to stop the soil from being washed out while you are watering. Liners can be home-made from a piece of plastic cut to size, with a layer of moss tucked between the basket and the plastic for a more decorative look. Alternatively, you can use a proprietary liner made from paper pulp or coconut matting. These come in a variety of shapes and sizes to adapt to all varieties of basket.

Whatever type of container you choose, it needs to be filled with a good compost (soil mix). Adding slow-release fertilizer granules and water-retaining granules can also help to promote luscious results.

■ OPPOSITE
A hanging basket successfully raises the height of the garden, and blends the flowers and foliage with garden buildings in a way that planted flowers or stand-alone containers can never do.

■ BELOW
There is no reason why hanging baskets should contain only flowers: the basket on the left contains wild strawberries, while the basket on the right has been planted productively with fresh herbs.

Hanging Gardens

An alternative to a conventional hanging basket is to design your planting so that the basket or container is made part of the display. Ordinary shopping baskets, buckets, agricultural containers, even kitchen equipment such as colanders, pots and pans with drainage holes drilled in the base, can all be used as hanging baskets with character.

If your chosen container is large and might possibly become too heavy when planted to be suspended, a useful trick is to put a layer of broken-up expanded polystyrene (left over from plant trays or the packaging around electrical goods) in the bottom of the container. This is lighter than the equivalent amount of compost (soil mix) and will provide good drainage for the plants.

■ ABOVE
A witty interpretation of a hanging basket, this Indian birdcage makes an ideal receptacle for potted plants. Hung in a mulberry tree, it lends floral interest in early spring before the leaves have burst from their buds.

■ ABOVE
Free-standing, miniature mangers, stacked one over the other, make a vibrant column of colour in a tiny courtyard garden.

■ ABOVE
The most unlikely items can be used as hanging baskets. This pretty metal lantern from the Middle East has been filled with terracotta pots planted with variegated ivies to make a surprising and decorative hanging feature.

Summer Basket

Hanging baskets are summer favourites in even the smallest gardens, bringing a floral splash – and fragrance if you choose appropriate plants – to walls, verandas, patios and even basement areas. Plant them early in the year, once the threat of late frosts has passed, to give the plants time to "get their toes in" and fill out.

Tools and Materials

- hanging basket with chains or rope
- coconut fibre liner
- compost (soil mix)
- trowel
- water-retaining granules
- slow-release fertilizer granules
- 6 variegated ivies
- 2 diascia
- 6 verbenas
- watering can

1 Line the basket with the coconut fibre liner and part-fill with compost (soil mix), adding water-retaining and fertilizer granules as you go, according to the manufacturer's instructions.

2 Knock the ivy plants out of their pots and thread them through the sides of the basket. Place a diascia at either end of the basket. Add the verbenas.

3 Press more compost around each plant and down the sides of the basket so that everything is firmly bedded in. Water generously and hang the basket.

■ BELOW
Verbena and diascia, with their trailing, wiry stems and pretty colouring, make an unrestrained combination that will quickly clothe this basket. The variegated ivy provides a foundation of foliage to offset the colours of the flowers.

Ideas for Containers

Almost any interesting receptacle will make a container for plants; in fact, the more unusual it is, the more impact it will create. Once you begin to see the potential in tins, boxes, baskets and jars, you'll be motivated to create really original plantings. Here are some ideas to get you started.

■ OPPOSITE
In China, glazed pots are frequently used as small ponds in courtyards. This pot contains a water lily, a flowering rush and an aurum lily.

■ LEFT
With a couple of coats of varnish, an old wooden wine case will make an attractive and durable container for a miniature herb garden, which you could keep on the kitchen windowsill or near the back door, ready for use.

■ BELOW LEFT
Plant a kitchen garden in a selection of decorative oil cans, choosing a variety of sizes for a better show. These old cans have been planted with marjoram, nasturtiums, parsley, sage and borage.

■ BELOW
A flowerpot covered in mosaic makes an original container. This pot has been planted with miniature roses to match the flower motif design. A hole drilled into the base allows for drainage.

■ RIGHT
This large, sturdy cooking pot – found in a junk shop for next to nothing – makes a characterful container for plants.

POTTED HERB GARDEN

The use of time-honoured herbal remedies is enjoying renewed popularity as we come to appreciate the healing power of herbs. Here, herbs are planted in terracotta pots embellished with their botanical names and grouped together in a large saucer as a tribute to the apothecaries of old. Marigold, thyme, feverfew, lavender and rosemary have been used here, but you can vary the herbs according to what is available.

TOOLS AND MATERIALS

permanent marker pen

5 x 10cm/4in terracotta pots

selection of herbs: pot marigold (*Calendula*), thyme (*Thymus*), feverfew (*Matricaria*), lavender (*Lavandula*) and rosemary (*Rosmarinus*)

compost (soil mix) (optional)

terracotta saucer 36cm/14in in diameter

clay granules or gravel

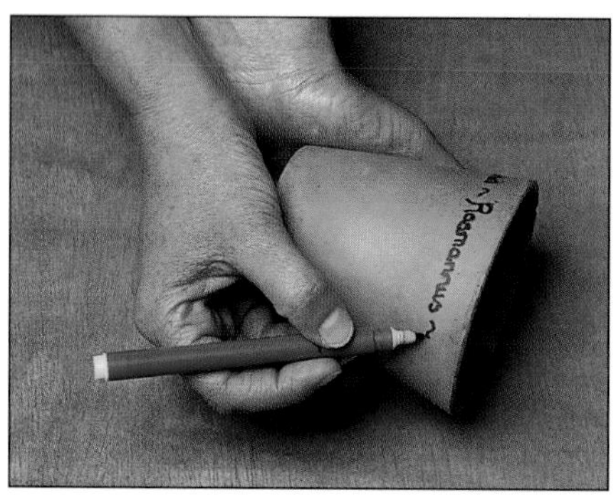

1 Use the marker pen to write the botanical plants' names around the rims of the pots. Plant the herbs with additional compost (soil mix) if necessary.

2 Fill the saucer with clay granules or gravel and arrange the pots on top.

■ BELOW

Thyme, one of the useful herbs in this potted arrangement, can be drunk as a refreshing tisane to aid digestion.

HERBAL REMEDIES

Feverfew: a leaf rolled into a ball of bread can be taken for the symptoms of migraine

Lavender: the essential oil is known to be an effective treatment for minor burns

Pot marigold: a healing and mildly antiseptic herb

Rosemary: use in an infusion for scalp problems; makes an excellent hair rinse

Thyme: drunk as a tisane, purifying and disinfectant

Bouquet Garni Display

The classic bouquet garni consists of parsley, thyme and a bay leaf tied into a posy with string. It is used to impart flavour to stews, soups and sauces. In Provence, rosemary is always added as well. In all but the coldest areas, it is possible to gather these herbs fresh for most of the year. Here, the herbs have been planted in a small, moss-lined wooden crate, which would sit quite happily outdoors, on the kitchen windowsill. Planting containers along a theme in this way makes a delightful compromise between the useful and the decorative. Keep a small stock of the herbs to be dried for use mid-winter.

Tools and Materials

- drill
- wooden crate, 25 x 20 x 15cm/10 x 8 x 6in
- 40cm/16in sisal rope
- permanent marker pen
- paintbrush
- liquid seaweed plant food
- moss
- small bay tree
- thyme
- 2 parsley plants
- compost (soil mix)
- coarse grit

1 To make the handles, drill two holes in each end of the wooden crate. Thread the ends of a 20cm/8in length of rope through each of the holes from the outside and tie a knot in the ends to secure.

2 Use the permanent marker pen to write on each side of the crate. Paint the wood with an equal mixture of liquid seaweed plant food and water, to give it a weathered appearance.

3 Line the crate with moss and plant the herbs in a mixture of three parts compost (soil mix) to one part coarse grit. Tuck more moss around the plants and water thoroughly.

■ BELOW
The ingredients of the traditional bouquet garni will grow happily outside the kitchen window, within easy reach of the cook.

Topiary Herbs

This is one of the most attractive and stylish ways to grow herbs, especially when they are planted in long-tom pots, which complete the sculptural effect. The herbs suitable for this treatment are those with woody stems such as rosemary, lemon verbena, santolina and lavender.

■ OPPOSITE
To display a group of potted herbs to greatest effect, stand them against a plain background so that their shapes are clearly outlined.

Select young plants with a strong, straight central stem, which can be trimmed to create the topiary shape. Once established, provided the herbs are regularly fed and watered and moved into larger pots as they grow, they should reach a good size and live for a number of years. A large plant trained like this would make a perfect centrepiece for a formal herb garden.

Bear in mind that the shape of long-tom pots makes them dry out more quickly than conventional pots, so frequent watering is essential. Prune the herbs every two weeks during the growing season. In colder areas, the plants will need winter protection, so pack them, pots and all, into a large wooden box filled with bark and stand them in a light, frost-free place.

Tools and Materials

- scissors
- young herb plants: rosemary, lavender, santolina or lemon verbena
- long-tom pots
- compost (soil mix)
- coarse grit
- washed gravel

1 Use the scissors to trim any side shoots from the central stem of each plant and to remove the foliage from the bottom half to two-thirds of the stem.

2 Trim the remaining foliage to shape. Transplant the herbs into terracotta pots using a mixture of two parts compost (soil mix) to one part coarse grit. Cover the compost with a layer of gravel. Water and stand in a sheltered, sunny position.

■ ABOVE
When the bloom of your summer roses has passed, cut the stems and stick into florist's foam for a topiary display.

Alpine Shell Garden

Create an alpine garden in a shell-decorated container for an unusual window box or garden decoration. The garden needs to be planted in spring after the frosts; once planted, it will need very little attention, producing masses of little flowers in summer in return for the occasional watering. It will rest in the winter, ready to grow with renewed vigour the following spring.

■ OPPOSITE
Choose alpine plants with small leaves and flowers to suit the miniature scale of this tiny garden-in-a-box.

Tools and Materials

- wooden vegetable box
- lime green emulsion (latex) paint
- paintbrush
- selection of about 8 alpine plants such as sempervivum, sedum and saxifrage
- glue gun
- 12 scallop shells
- large plastic bag
- scissors
- compost (soil mix)
- selection of shells

1 Paint the box with lime green emulsion (latex) paint and let dry. This paint is really meant for indoor use, and will weather down in time to give softer tones. Water the plants thoroughly and allow to drain.

2 Using the glue gun, attach scallop shells all around the sides of the box. Line the box with plastic cut from a large bag, and make drainage holes in it using scissors.

3 Fill the box with a layer of compost (soil mix), then arrange the large shells on top.

4 Remove the plants from their pots and position them in the box. The roots can be wedged under a shell and bedded well into the compost.

5 Water the box thoroughly. Until the plants grow to fill the box, you can add a few more small shells to cover the bare earth, if you like.

Decorating Pots

Transforming an ordinary flower pot into something special really doesn't have to be difficult. There are so many media to choose from that it is an easy matter to find one that suits your decorative style. You may be happy with paint applied in bold geometric patterns or simple motifs. If you are skilled with a paintbrush, you might like to try something a little more figurative. Another easy option is to glue decorations on to your pots – ceramic chips, perhaps, to make a mosaic, or shells arranged in a simple textural pattern.

■ BELOW
This impressive garden urn is decorated with modern faces but has a look that is reminiscent of Byzantine icons. It will add a touch of grandeur to even the dullest corner of the garden or patio.

■ RIGHT
If you break a favourite plate or dish, this is a delightful way to continue to enjoy its colour and pattern. Use ceramic chips in co-ordinated colours and simple patterns to make striking mosaic pots.

■ BELOW
This pot has been given a necklace of weathered glass "beads" dangling on wires from a wire ring fixed under the rim of the pot.

STENCILLED TERRACOTTA POT

Cheap terracotta pots can be made to look stylish and distinctive using simple stencilled designs. Choose paint colours that will enhance your plants and look good within your garden colour-scheme. Terracotta is porous and will absorb a lot of paint, so you may need several coats, depending on the colour you are using.

TOOLS AND MATERIALS

- tape measure
- terracotta pot
- chalk
- ruler
- masking tape
- artist's acrylic paints
- stencil brush
- acetate stencils

1 Measure the circumference of the pot at the top and bottom and divide into equal sections. Join each of these points with a vertical chalk line.

2 Mask off the outlines of the background shapes using masking tape and then paint. Add further coats as necessary and allow to dry.

3 Tape the stencil to the pot and apply several coats of paint. Move the stencil around the rim of the pot and repeat to complete the design.

■ BELOW
Once you have gained some confidence with simple stencils, experiment with freehand designs and other techniques such as sponging, stippling and dragging. Try other types of paint for different effects, such as metallic paints.

Mexican Painted Pots

Rings of folk-art motifs painted over stripes of vibrant colours give simple pots a rich Mexican look. This looks best if you leave some stripes of unpainted terracotta, and the style suits pots with fluted tops especially well. Stacked together and planted up with pelargoniums in hot summer colours, they make a lively garden feature.

Tools and Materials

- terracotta pot with fluted top
- masking tape
- scissors
- white undercoat
- paintbrushes
- gouache poster colours
- semi-gloss polyurethane varnish
- varnish brush

1 Mark the stripes on the pot using masking tape. Cut some lengths into narrower widths to give variations in the finished design. Bear in mind that the areas covered with masking tape will remain natural terracotta.

2 Paint the main body of the pot, below the rim, with white undercoat. When dry, paint in the coloured stripes, changing the colour for each band. Leave to dry.

3 When the paint is completely dry, carefully peel off the masking tape.

4 Using a fine brush and the white undercoat, paint a series of traditional motifs along the stripes. When completely dry, coat with varnish.

■ OPPOSITE
The hot colours of these painted pots will hold their own in the sunniest spot on the patio. Fill them with vividly coloured flowering plants or exotic-looking succulents.

Painting a Borage Bucket

There is an old country saying that "a garden without borage is a garden without courage", which refers to the old herbalists' belief that this plant has the ability to lift the spirits. In addition to its medicinal properties – its oil is as potent as that of evening primrose – its pretty, blue, cucumber-scented flowers will gladden the heart when added to a glass of summer punch or used to decorate a salad.

■ OPPOSITE
Beautiful blue borage flowers look great against the silvery grey of a galvanized bucket. Here, they pick up the blue stencilled design on the watering can.

Tools and Materials

- pencil
- stencil cardboard
- craft knife
- cutting mat
- masking tape
- galvanized bucket, 18cm/7in in diameter
- artist's acrylic paints in mid-blue, deep blue and white
- stencil brush
- fine paintbrush
- polyurethane varnish
- varnish brush
- borage plants

1 Draw two or three borage flowers on a piece of stencil cardboard and cut out the outlines with a craft knife to make a stencil. Attach the stencil to the side of the bucket, using masking tape, and paint the flowers in mid-blue in an overlapping random pattern.

2 Using a fine paintbrush, add details to the flowers in deep blue and white. Protect the decoration with a coat of polyurethane varnish and let it dry before adding the borage plants.

■ RIGHT
The borage plant motif can make even the most practical of gardening equipment look charming. Adapt the idea for other pieces, perhaps painting them with other simple flowers such as daisies or pansies.

VERDIGRIS BUCKET

There is something irresistible about the luminous, subtle blue-green tones of verdigris. It is a colour that always complements plants and it is not difficult to reproduce on an ordinary galvanized bucket. Alternatively, you can use the same painting technique, substituting rust-coloured acrylic for aqua, to produce a rusted effect.

TOOLS AND MATERIALS

medium-grade sandpaper
galvanized bucket
metal primer
paintbrushes
gold emulsion (latex) paint
amber shellac
artist's acrylic paint in white and aqua-green
natural sponge
polyurethane varnish
varnish brush

■ LEFT
The pale, cool aqua tone of verdigris makes a wonderful foil for these delicate and velvety dark violas.

1 Sand the bucket, then prime with metal primer and allow to dry. Paint with gold paint and leave the bucket to dry for at least 2–3 hours.

2 Paint the bucket with amber shellac and let dry. Mix white acrylic with aqua-green to make the verdigris, and thin it to a watery consistency.

3 Sponge the verdigris paint over the shellac and allow to dry for 1–2 hours before applying a coat of varnish.

LEAD CHIMNEY

Lead has been used to make garden containers for centuries, and its chalky blue-grey tones look wonderful with plants. But lead is incredibly heavy and very expensive, so here is a way of faking it, using a plastic chimney and a simple paint effect.

■ LEFT
A lead-coloured container looks stunning filled with silvery foliage and pale flowers.

TOOLS AND MATERIALS

- sandpaper
- plastic, terracotta-coloured chimney
- acrylic primer
- paintbrushes
- emulsion (latex) paint in charcoal grey and white
- acrylic scumble glaze
- polyurethane varnish
- varnish brush

1 Sand the chimney to give a key for the paint. Paint with one coat of acrylic primer and leave to dry for 1–2 hours.

2 Apply a coat of charcoal grey emulsion (latex) and leave to dry for 2–3 hours.

3 Tint some scumble glaze with white emulsion and thin with water. Paint over the chimney randomly using a large artist's paintbrush. Blend the colour by washing over the surface with a wet brush and leave to dry.

4 Add more of the white scumble mixture to parts of the chimney to "age" the surface. Leave to dry, then paint with a coat of polyurethane varnish.

Tin-can Plant Nursery

Seedlings can be decorative in themselves, so pick them out from their seed trays into a collection of tin cans mounted on a wall plaque. They can grow on there, sheltered by the wall and high above any threatening late frosts, until they are ready to be planted out. The plaque itself looks wonderful made from ordinary tinned steel cans, but if you want to add a bit more colour, scour delicatessens for vividly printed cans.

■ OPPOSITE
Printed and plain tin cans take on a new and more interesting appearance when they are massed together on a Mediterranean blue wall panel.

Tools and Materials

- wooden board about 60 x 30cm/24 x 12in
- undercoat
- paintbrush
- blue gloss paint
- variety of empty cans with paper labels removed
- can opener
- tin snips
- pliers
- hammer
- nail
- tacks

1 Paint the board with a coat of undercoat and one or two coats of gloss paint, allowing each coat to dry before applying the next.

2 Stand the cans open end down and, using the can opener, cut round half of the bottom.

3 Using tin snips, cut open the side of the can to make two equal flaps.

4 Open out the sides with pliers and snip a V-shape into each one. Bend up the can bottom in line with the sides. Pierce the bottom of each can by hammering a nail through it.

5 Arrange all the cans on the board, then tack them in place, hammering a tack through each point of the side flaps.

Dea
Dea
Dea
White Tower
ΟΜΟΣΠΟΝΔΙΑΣ
OMOSPONDIAS
THESSALONIKI
GREECE - GRIECHENLAND
NETTO

Moss and Netting Urn

This rustic urn is created from nothing more remarkable than chicken wire and moss: a collection of these elegant containers would make wonderful garden decorations for a special occasion, flanking steps or ranged along a balustrade. Even without the moss filling, the wire shape makes a quirky sculpture in itself. When the urns are not in use, they will keep their colour longer if they are kept in a dark place, as moss fades quite quickly in daylight.

Tools and Materials

- wire cutters
- chicken wire
- moss
- florist's wire
- 20cm/8in plastic pot

1 Cut a 1.5m/1½yd length of chicken wire. Fold it in half so that the raw edges meet and pack a layer of moss between the layers of wire.

2 Fold the chicken wire and moss "sandwich" in half lengthways and join the edges securely together with lengths of florist's wire.

3 Slip the plastic pot into the top end of the tube (the end with no rough edges) and form the lip of the urn by folding the chicken wire outwards from the rim of the pot.

4 Leaving the pot in place, firmly squeeze the chicken wire with both hands just below the pot to make the stem of the urn.

5 Make the base by folding the rough edges in and squeezing and squashing the wire into the desired shape. Stand the urn up periodically while you do this to check that it is level.

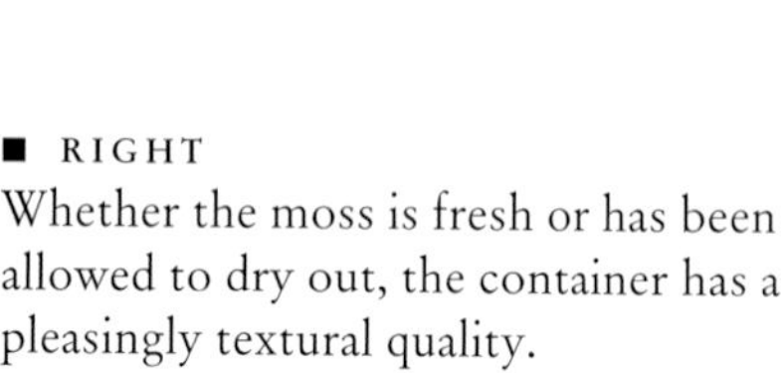

■ RIGHT
Whether the moss is fresh or has been allowed to dry out, the container has a pleasingly textural quality.

EARTHY PAINTED POTS

Liquid seaweed plant food is a wonderful rich brown colour and can be diluted and painted on to terracotta pots to encourage the growth of moss and give the appearance of age. Undiluted, the colour is very deep and looks beautiful as a decoration for terracotta. You can either preserve this rich colour with a coat of varnish or you could leave the pots unsealed: most of the coating will be worn away by the weather if the pots are left outside, leaving soft faded patterns, like traces of ancient frescoes.

TOOLS AND MATERIALS

masking tape
terracotta pots
liquid seaweed plant food
paintbrushes
matt polyurethane varnish
varnish brush

1 Use masking tape to protect the areas of the pot that you want to remain unpainted. Brush liquid seaweed plant food on to the unmasked areas and leave to dry completely.

2 Peel off the masking tape and seal the whole pot with a coat of matt varnish, if you wish to retain the rich brown colour.

■ ABOVE
Beautiful pots in rich natural hues of terracotta and earthy dark brown hold a winter arrangement of twigs and cones.

Garden Decorations and Accessories

Now comes the icing on the cake and the finishing touch: when your garden is looking a picture and you really want to draw attention to its design and its planting, add some well-judged artefacts to draw the eye or raise a smile for a truly decorated garden.

Decorating your outdoor room is enormous fun. Allow yourself to be idiosyncratic in your choice of embellishments. An antique metal birdcage may seem incongruous to the garden landscape but, if festooned with flowers, it can become a wonderfully original feature. Mobiles and wind chimes look delightful and produce gentle chimes to soothe the ear, while a customized birdhouse will attract bird life to your garden and help to support the birds through the winter months. If you're looking to add romance to your garden, hang a few decorative hearts here and there.

■ ABOVE
Galvanized metal artefacts work best dotted casually about the garden.

■ OPPOSITE
Whether it is fruit, vegetables or seedlings you want to protect, make a scarecrow to double as an amusing garden sculpture. This dapper chap with a colander face wears a denim jacket and a sporty panama hat.

GARDEN SCULPTURE

The classic garden decoration is sculpture: for centuries, stone statues, busts and fountains have graced formal gardens, providing focal points or charming surprises in secluded spots. Classic figures are still popular as reproductions, along with baroque-style cherubs and the little imps known as *putti*.

■ RIGHT
An exquisite male torso, turned modestly towards the wall, contributes art and structure at a secluded side of the garden.

Original stone statues, aged by lichens, natural salts and the passage of time, obscuring detail and combining to create an authentic patina, are exquisite but prohibitively expensive. Economic alternatives are available, however: accelerate the aging process on modern stone copies by coating them with live yogurt and keeping them in damp, shady places.

MODERN VALUES

Beautiful as the traditional forms of sculpture are, contemporary alternatives may be more relevant to your garden and far more personal to you. Metal and wire sculpture is fashionable nowadays and works very well outside, as does willow, woven into dynamic figures. Mosaic, too, can be a lovely medium for sculpture as it quickly transforms all sorts of unpromising bits of paraphernalia. Plants themselves can become sculpture in the form of topiary, where small-leaved evergreens are clipped into spirals, cones, orbs or animals. It is a slow process as the shrubs take time to grow, but some garden centres sell them already started, so all you have to do is keep them trimmed to shape.

■ ABOVE
Metal and water combine in a fascinating, dynamic sculpture that is a cross between a birdbath and a water feature.

■ LEFT
Even a rusty old chair frame can become sculpture. This one, flanked on two sides by neatly trimmed trees, is given throne-like importance.

■ LEFT
Old galvanized baths and bowls have been light-heartedly decorated with mosaic cut from broken china, plus a couple of old teacups and some ginger-jar tops.

■ ABOVE
Classical Roman and Greek statues make elegant focal points, set at the end of vistas.

■ LEFT
Tradtional sculpture, such as this stone urn, gives an austere sense of formality to the garden design, and would add something of a regal touch to a large sweeping garden.

■ RIGHT
Positioned down the length of the garden, pots and containers can create a visual feast that is less formal than traditional garden sculpture.

■ RIGHT
Topiary is making a comeback, and clever trimming will help to keep its effect strictly contemporary.

OUTDOOR DECORATIONS

Sculpture is the classic outdoor art form, but if you don't have money to spend on garden decorations or if the space in your garden is limited, then there are plenty of alternatives. You can use anything that adds structure and form to the garden.

Large plant pots and boxes are decorative as well as functional. The traditional example is the classic urn, but you don't even have to go that far. Ordinary pots, painted or carefully arranged in groups, can make a statement, as can novel containers. Think of some unusual hanging baskets, such as colanders, baskets or buckets, or gather potted plants into a spectacular container, such as an old wheelbarrow, to make a display. You can add more purely decorative ideas, such as whirligigs, wind chimes, driftwood or pebble collections. Or you can fashion your own decorations – motifs such as hearts or stars made from twigs and branches, wire or raffia.

■ OPPOSITE
An old wicker mannequin teamed with a miniature wirework version makes an amusing and unexpected decoration.

■ ABOVE
A collection of limpet shell rings hung on strong threads makes an attractive, joyous wind chime.

■ ABOVE
This inexpensive, painted bamboo birdcage, filled with potted pinks, makes a charming ornament.

■ LEFT
Even simple galvanized shapes take on decorative appeal: all they need is a couple of coats of paint.

Decorative Mosaic Spheres

Mosaic spheres inspired by millefiori African beadwork would make unusual garden decorations. Based on wooden or polystyrene balls, they can be decorated with broken china, glass mosaic tiles or fragments of mirror. If you use a polystyrene foundation, the spheres will be quite light and could be hung in a tree.

■ BELOW
Mosaic stars dotted amongst the foliage can add an element of surprise to a blooming hedge of roses.

Tools and Materials

- polystyrene or wooden spheres
- PVA (white) glue
- paintbrush
- pencil
- selection of old china
- mirror
- tile nippers
- rubber gloves
- waterproof tile adhesive
- powdered waterproof tile grout
- vinyl matt emulsion (latex) or acrylic paint
- nailbrush
- soft cloth

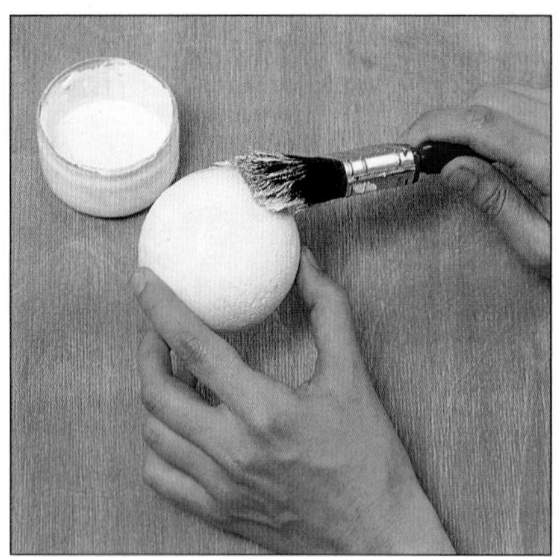

1 Seal the polystyrene or wooden spheres with diluted PVA (white) glue. Leave to dry.

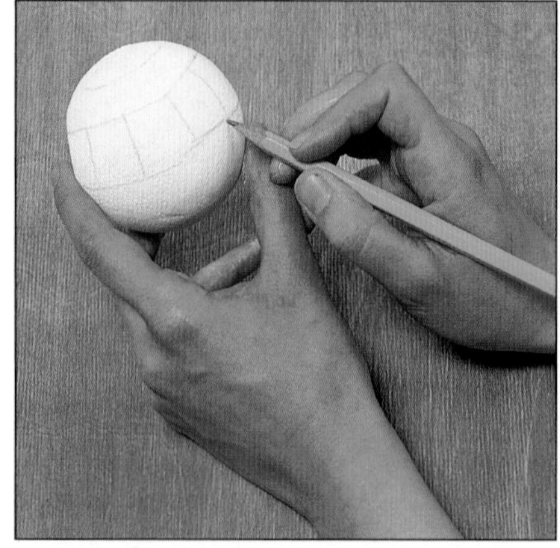

2 Using a pencil, draw a simple design on a sphere. A combination of circular shapes works well, but experiment with other geometric shapes and abstract designs.

3 Cut the china and mirror into different sized pieces using tile nippers. Stick the pieces to the sphere using waterproof tile adhesive. Leave overnight to dry.

■ RIGHT
Position the spheres to suggest bowls mid-game for a fun and very modern ornamental display.

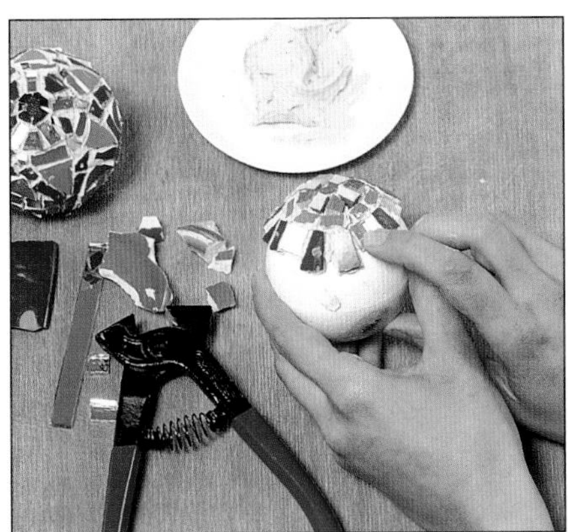

4 Mix powdered grout with water and use a little vinyl matt emulsion (latex) or acrylic paint to colour it. Wearing rubber gloves, rub the grout into the surface of the sphere, filling all the cracks between the tesserae.

5 Leave for a few minutes until the surface has dried, then brush off excess grout using a stiff nailbrush.

6 Leave to dry overnight, then polish with a soft dry cloth.

Outdoor Frames

There's no reason why garden walls should not be decorated with pictures, just as you would the walls of a room, whether they are merely glimpsed through a curtain of foliage and flowers or provide the focus of interest on an unclothed wall.

Stone, metal or tiled plaques can be fixed to the walls, but pictures in frames also have a place. The frames themselves should be weatherproof, so the most appropriate material to use is wood that has already been aged and hardened by the weather. You could recycle lengths of timber from old fencing or garden furniture, or collect some beautiful, bleached driftwood from the beach. To fill the frames, put together collages of natural subjects that will be perfectly in keeping with the garden: an arrangement of leaves or soft downy feathers; shells collected on holiday, or a mosaic decoration made from broken pieces of patterned china or shop-bought tesserae. As an alternative, you could frame an old mirror and hang it cleverly from an accommodating branch or prop it in a niche in a wall, to visually expand the space, giving the impression of another garden beyond the wall.

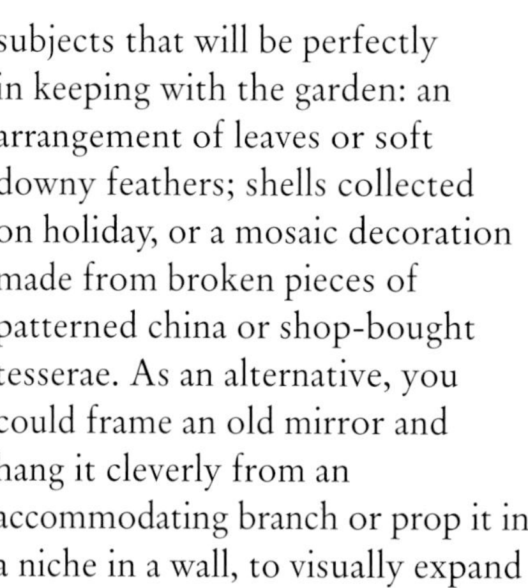

■ BELOW
The muted, weathered tones and contorted shapes of driftwood just beg to be used. Here, a shabby old mirror frame has been transformed using the curved edge of an old garden table for the top and various pieces of driftwood to make a wonderful organic decoration, quite in keeping with its surroundings.

■ ABOVE
This green and twiggy frame will give your outdoor room a log cabin touch. Artificial grass, available from modelmaker's suppliers, was glued to a piece of hardboard before the twigs were added in a lattice design.

■ LEFT
Neatly tailored male pheasant feathers look wonderful in ordered lines. The soft grey tones of this frame, made of wood recycled from an old barn door, are echoed in the down on the feathers.

■ RIGHT
Cover the outside edge of a mirror with a rich collection of shells and coral, glued in position, for an outdoor frame with an inimitable touch of seashore style.

■ RIGHT
This recycled picture frame celebrates the beauty of weathered timber. The wonderful texture and colour mean that the frame is easily enhanced with pebbles, string and seaweed to make a naturally organic picture.

China Tiles

If you want to use mosaic as a garden decoration but are daunted by a large-scale project, you could try making some of these small one-off tiles. Try out simple patterns, using a selection of broken china, and think of the tiles as sketches or experiments before embarking on more complex mosaics.

■ OPPOSITE
These mosaic tiles could be displayed singly or in groups, stuck on a garden wall or used to decorate a table.

Tools and Materials

- plain white tiles
- PVA (white) glue
- paintbrush
- pencil
- selection of old china
- tile nippers
- tile adhesive
- acrylic paint or cement dye
- powdered waterproof tile grout
- rubber gloves
- nailbrush
- soft cloth

1 Prime the back of a plain tile with diluted PVA (white) glue and leave to dry. Draw a simple design on the back of the tile using a pencil.

2 Cut a selection of china into small pieces that will fit into your design, using tile nippers. Arrange the tesserae in groups according to colour and shape.

3 Dip the tesserae into tile adhesive and press them, one by one, on to the tile, using the drawing as a guide. When the tile is completely covered, leave it to dry overnight.

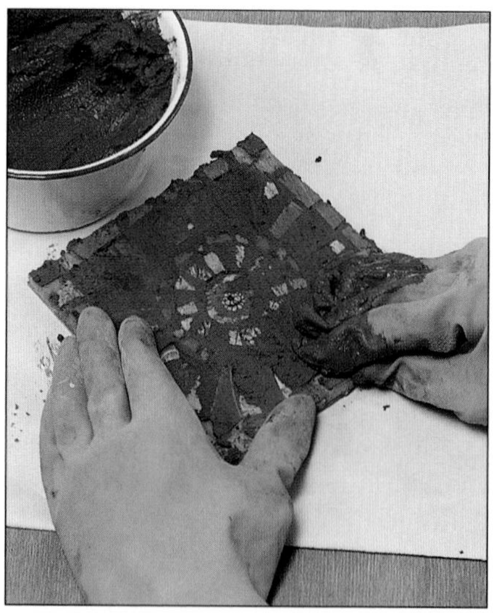

4 Mix acrylic paint or cement dye with powdered waterproof tile grout. Add a little water and mix to a dough-like consistency. Wearing rubber gloves, rub the grout into the surface of the mosaic, making sure that all the gaps are filled. Leave to dry for about ten minutes.

5 Scrub the surface of the tile with a stiff nailbrush to remove all the excess grout, then leave the tile to dry for 24 hours. Polish the surface with a soft dry cloth.

Mosaic Clock

This clockface is decorated with mosaic made from hand-painted Mexican tiles. While the painting on the tiles is very free, and they have been cut into uneven shapes, the resulting tesserae are used to construct a precise geometric design that draws attention to the positions of the hands, making it easy to read the time. The base of the clock is made from two pieces of wood, with a hole cut into the thick piece at the back to accommodate the clock mechanism and batteries. The clock can live outdoors, but position it in a sheltered place, where it will receive the maximum amount of protection from the weather.

Tools and Materials

- 4mm/⅛in plywood
- 2cm/¾in chipboard
- compasses
- marker pen or pencil
- ruler
- jigsaw
- drill and bits
- clock movement and hands
- PVA (white) glue
- paintbrush
- strong wood glue
- 4 clamps or heavy weights
- tile nippers
- selection of plain and patterned tiles
- cement-based tile adhesive
- shells
- flexible (putty) knife
- rubber gloves
- sponge
- sandpaper
- soft cloth

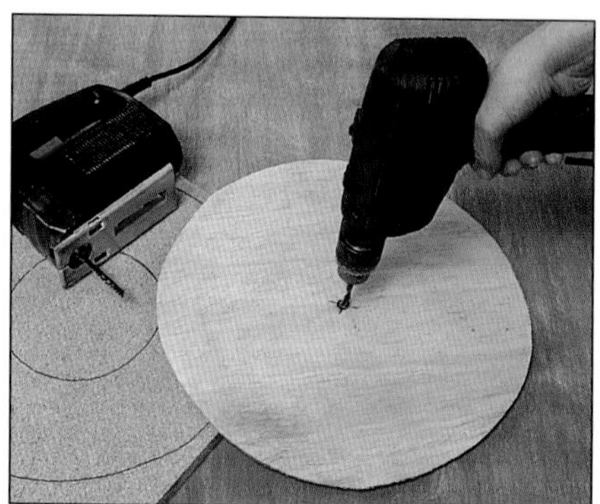

1 Draw a 40cm/16in circle on both the plywood and the chipboard, and cut out with the jigsaw . Drill a hole through the centre of the chipboard circle large enough to take the jigsaw blade. Saw a hole to accommodate the clock mechanism and batteries. Drill a hole through the centre of the plywood circle for the spindle. Prime both pieces with diluted PVA (white) glue and let dry.

2 Stick the plywood and chipboard circles together using strong wood glue. Clamp the pieces together or leave under heavy weights overnight to dry.

3 Draw a circle in the centre of the plywood circle with a radius of the length of the minute hand. Using a marker pen or pencil, divide the face into quarters and use these as the basis for your design.

4 Using tile nippers, cut the patterned tiles into small irregular shapes. This design uses tiles in three different patterns, to differentiate the areas of the clockface. Stick the tiles on with cement-based tile adhesive, making sure they lie flat.

5 Cut plain tiles into small rectangular shapes for the rim of the clock. Tile the border, marking the positions of the quarter hours. When attaching the shells, make sure they are positioned so that they will not obstruct the movement of the clock hands.

6 Use a flexible (putty) knife to smooth tile adhesive around the rim of the clock. Wearing rubber gloves, work the adhesive over the clockface, making sure all the gaps are filled. Wipe clean with a sponge and leave to dry for approximately 24 hours.

7 Sand off any excess cement and polish with a soft dry cloth.

8 Attach the clock, fitting the movement and batteries into the hole at the back. Insert the spindle through the central hole and fit the hands.

■ RIGHT
Simple groups of pretty shells have been used to mark the quarter hours on this clockface.

BIRDHOUSES

Birds are the most welcome of garden visitors. They are fascinating to watch, delightful to listen to, and earn their keep by eating garden pests such as snails and aphids. Nowadays, as the natural habitats of many species diminish, even quite small gardens can provide an important proportion of their territories, and they won't need much encouragement.

■ OPPOSITE
A charming, scaled-down dovecote makes a tiny folly for a miniature garden in a trough or window box.

Encourage birds to visit your garden regularly with birdhouses, bird-feeding tables and baths. Seedheads left standing in the winter border and shrubs that bear berries such as cotoneaster and daphne ensure a winter food supply. Remember that if you feed garden birds in winter you must do so regularly, as they will come to depend on you.

Even better than garden visitors are permanent residents: bird-houses are rewarding to watch when occupied and will become garden features all year round.

Birds can be encouraged to make nests even in the most urban of areas, and if you provide a suitable nesting box they will both feed and breed in your garden. A bird's own choice of nesting place would be a sheltered spot, so take care to place your birdhouse away from possible disturbances, up a wall or tree trunk, and facing away from prevailing wind and rain.

■ ABOVE RIGHT
A whole row of basic birdhouses, painted in bright, contrasting colours looks like a row of smart beach huts.

■ RIGHT
A New England-style clapboard house for upwardly mobile birds: mount the house on a stout post and site it out of reach of overhanging trees if cats frequent the garden.

CUSTOMIZED NESTING BOX

Ready-made nesting boxes are available in every shape and size, but a simple box can be transformed with a lick of paint and a few decorative touches. This house is painted in Shaker style and finished with a finial cut from scrap timber and an apple twig for a perch. To ensure that a nesting box gives you maximum pleasure, position it so that you will be able to see it from a window when you are indoors as well as when you are out in the garden.

TOOLS AND MATERIALS

- nesting box
- vinyl matt emulsion (latex) paint in 2 colours
- paintbrush
- marker pen
- decorative finial
- PVA (white) glue
- drill
- apple twig

1 Paint the box with emulsion (latex) paint in the first colour and leave to dry. Draw the door shape and the heart motifs using a marker pen.

2 Fill in the design and paint the finial with the second colour of emulsion paint and leave to dry completely.

3 Glue the finial in place at the front of the roof ridge using PVA (white) glue. Drill a hole to fit the apple twig beneath the entrance hole. Apply glue to the twig and push it into position.

■ OPPOSITE
Hang this pretty nesting box where the birds will be safe from predators; they will be happier if there is some overhanging foliage to give them a little shelter and privacy.

■ LEFT
If your birds would prefer a more metropolitan dwelling, paint a ready-made nesting box blue-grey and roof it with copper foil. The door surround is also made from copper foil – bend this back on itself, not into the hole, so that there are no sharp edges around the entrance to the box.

Hanging Bird-feeding Table

If you put out food and fresh water regularly, your garden will soon become a haven for wild birds. The birds quickly get to know and will pass the word around to make your bird-feeding table a popular stopping-off point.

There is immense pleasure to be gained from watching the different species that come to feed daily. This bird-feeding table is made from rough timber, with a lip around the edge to stop nuts and seeds rolling off.

Tools and Materials

- 2 lengths of rough timber, 25 x 12.5 x 1cm/10 x 5½ x ½in
- 2 battens 25 x 2.5 x 2.5cm/ 10 x 1 x 1in
- nails
- hammer
- 4 battens 28 x 5 x 1cm/ 11 x 2 x ½in
- wood preservative
- small decorator's paintbrush
- pencil
- ruler
- 4 brass hooks
- scissors
- 2m/6½ft sisal string

1 To make the base of the table, lay the two lengths of rough timber side by side and place the 25cm/10in battens across the wood, one at each end. Nail the battens securely in place.

2 Nail the four 28cm/11in battens around the edges of the base, allowing a lip of at least 2.5cm/1in. Paint all the surfaces of the table with wood preservative and leave to dry.

3 Use a pencil and ruler to mark a point in each corner of the table. Screw in a brass hook on each of the points.

4 Cut the sisal string into four equal lengths and tie a small loop in one end of each piece. Attach each loop to a hook, then gather up the strings above the table and tie in a loop for hanging.

■ OPPOSITE
String is tied to a hook in each corner so that the table can be hung in a tree, out of reach of predators.

■ LEFT
Specialist bird seed suppliers can provide information about which types of seed will attract which particular species of bird.

Copper Birdbath

You will have endless pleasure watching the birds preening and cleaning in this beautiful, yet eminently practical, beaten copper birdbath. Maintain a constant supply of fresh drinking water all year round to ensure the health and happiness of the birds in your locality.

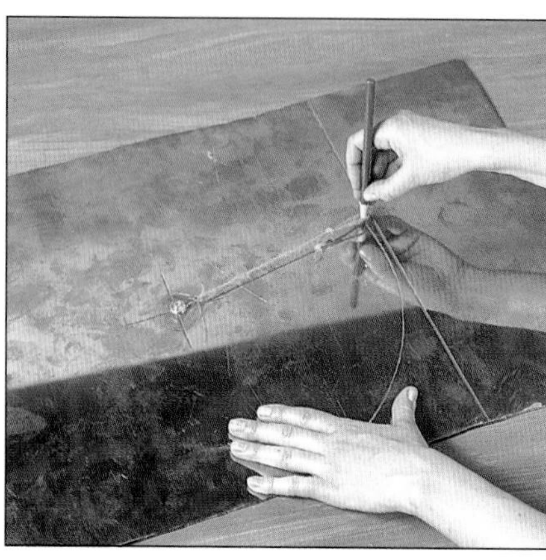

1 Using a chinagraph pencil and a piece of looped string, mark a 45cm/18in circle on the copper sheet.

2 Wearing protective gloves, cut out the circle with a pair of tin snips. Smooth the sharp edge using a file.

Tools and Materials

- chinagraph pencil
- string
- 9mm/⅜in 20 SWG copper sheet
- protective gloves
- tin snips
- file
- blanket
- hammer
- 4m/13ft medium copper wire
- bench vice
- strong hook
- slow-speed electric drill
- 3mm/⅛in bit

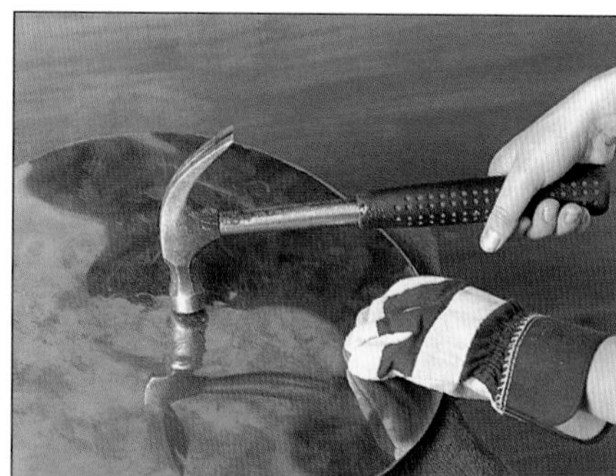

3 Lay the copper circle on a blanket and lightly hammer it from the centre. Spread the dips out to the rim. Repeat, starting in the centre each time, until you have the required shape. To make the perch, loop 1m/39in copper wire and hold the ends in a vice. Fasten a hook into the chuck of a drill. Put the hook through the loop and run the drill to twist the wire. Drill three holes, equally spaced, around the rim of the bath. Divide the remaining wire into three equal lengths and knot one end of each. Thread through the holes from beneath the bath. Slip the twisted wire over two straight wires to form a perch, and bend the tops of the wires together into a loop for hanging.

■ ABOVE
This elegant birdbath, with spare, modern lines, features a wire perch suspended over the water for the birds to stand on as they drink.

GAZEBO FEEDER

Constructed from a small glass lantern and some recycled tin cans, this little bird-feeder will hang like a jewel amongst the foliage of a tree.

TOOLS AND MATERIALS

- glass lantern
- tape measure
- thin glass
- chinagraph pencil
- try-square
- glass cutter
- ruler
- protective gloves
- shiny tin can, washed and dried
- tin snips
- flux and soldering iron
- solder
- try-square
- fine wire mesh

1 This lantern required extra glass to be installed. If this is the case with yours, measure the areas required and reduce all measurements by 6mm/¼in to allow for the metal border. Using a chinagraph pencil, mark the measurements on the glass, then cut out by running a glass cutter in a single pass along a ruler. Wearing protective gloves, tap along the line to break the glass. Cut 9mm/⅜in strips of metal from a tin can using tin snips.

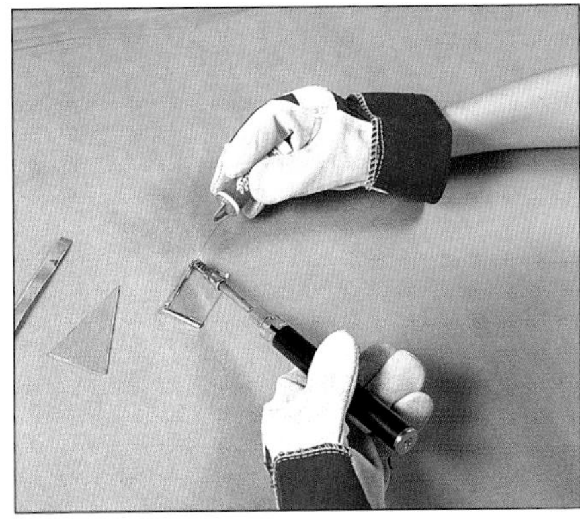

2 Wrap a strip of metal around each edge of each glass panel. Trim, then smear soldering flux on to the mating surfaces of each corner. Solder the corner joints of each panel. Heat a joint with a soldering iron and apply the solder. Remove the iron to allow the solder to cool and set.

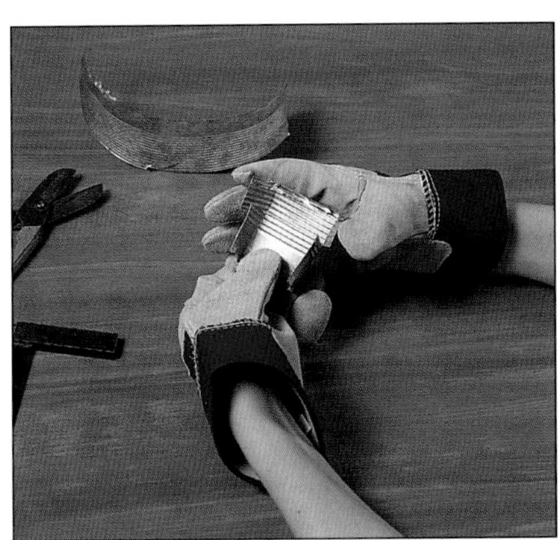

3 Measure the openings for the hoppers and fold sections of the tin can to suit, using a try-square or ruler to keep the fold lines straight. Solder the meeting points of each hopper. Cut out a platform from fine wire mesh and solder the platform, the panels and the hoppers in place on the framework.

■ BELOW
This sophisticated bird-feeder makes a delightful detail in a quiet garden corner.

FUNCTIONAL DECORATIONS

The very paraphernalia of gardening can be decorative. An old garden fork, its handle polished with use, a galvanized watering can, turned soft grey with time, or a wheelbarrow, pitted with wear, all have attractive forms that can give structure to the garden. Somehow, the balance and symmetry that good tools must possess in order to work efficiently usually also result in shapes that are easy on the eye. They have reassuring associations, too: they evoke a sense of outdoor life and remind us that people are nearby. So let them loiter around the garden; leave them where they were last used, and they will reward you with their spontaneous decorative appeal.

■ OPPOSITE
An old watering can, its curves reminiscent of a vintage car, provides a simple structural note left at the edge of a pathway.

■ BELOW
Sundials may not be moveable decorations, but their original *raison d'être* reminds us that these are not fripperies. They were clearly more necessary in centuries gone by than they are today, but they still exude a functional quality that is both honest and pleasing.

■ LEFT
Even old garden tools make decorative garden ornaments, left just where they were last used.

TWIGWAM

Plant supports are functional, but that doesn't mean they can't be decorative too. This one, made from branches pruned from garden trees interwoven with willow, makes a charming structural detail in a flower bed. Alternatively, it can be used to support clematis or any other climber for a wonderful, free-standing, outdoor floral display.

TOOLS AND MATERIALS

3 unbranched poles, about 90cm/3ft long

string or strands of willow

3 unbranched poles, about 30cm/12in long

plenty of fine, freshly cut willow branches

2 Stand the three shorter poles between the longer ones and tie them in the same way. Start to weave the willow branches in and out of the poles, working upwards from the bottom.

1 Stand up the three taller poles to form a "wigwam" and tie them together at the top with string or willow.

3 Once enough of the wigwam has been woven to keep the shorter poles securely in position, untie them. Continue weaving until the shorter poles are almost covered.

■ RIGHT
This woven willow support would look pretty entwined with sweet peas or nasturtiums, to give instant height in a summer border.

CHICKEN WIRE CLOCHE

This quirky chicken wire cloche can be used to protect plants from slugs and birds or can be simply "planted" into the flowerbed as a charming and original miniature obelisk.

TOOLS AND MATERIALS

- wire cutters
- fine-mesh chicken wire
- pliers
- medium-gauge garden wire

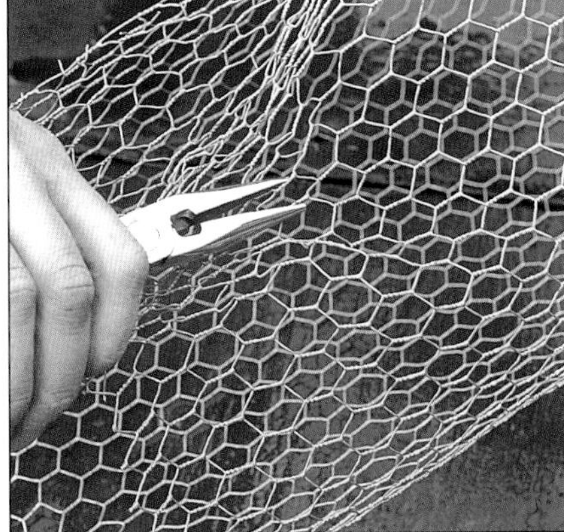

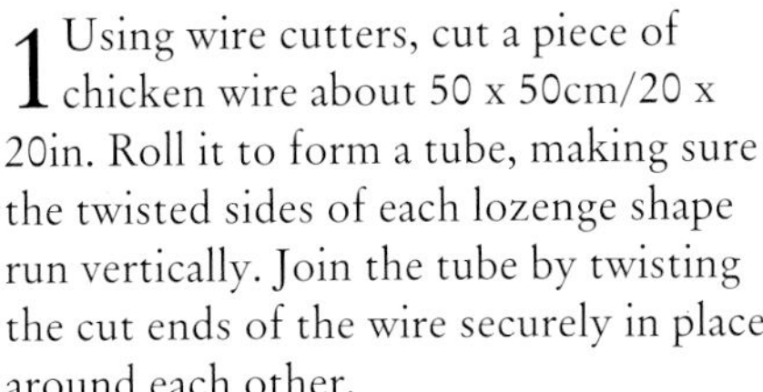

1 Using wire cutters, cut a piece of chicken wire about 50 x 50cm/20 x 20in. Roll it to form a tube, making sure the twisted sides of each lozenge shape run vertically. Join the tube by twisting the cut ends of the wire securely in place around each other.

2 Use the pliers to squeeze the wire into shape. At the top, squeeze each lozenge shape as tightly as it will go. Continue to pinch the wires together down the tube, squeezing each hole less and less until you reach the fullest part of the shape.

3 At the bottom of the cloche, make a "skirt" by narrowing the shape again, then letting it fan out gracefully. Wind garden wire tightly around the top to finish the cloche.

■ RIGHT
With a bit of original thought, you can turn an everyday material like chicken wire into an amusing miniature folly for the garden.

PRETTY EFFECTS IN PRACTICAL AREAS

Vegetable patches need not be the Cinderellas of the garden. There is something beautifully voluptuous about burgeoning fruits and first-class vegetables, and the structures they need to climb up can be very appealing. Make a virtue of your vegetable garden, whether you grow your produce in a separate part of the garden, or mix fruits and vegetables in amongst the plants in the flowerbeds.

■ OPPOSITE
Keeping track of plant labels can be practically impossible once the plants are growing and overflowing their original sites, so turn them into a decoration in themselves. Make a noticeboard from a piece of plywood, giving it a decorative motif at the top, such as these tulips. Paint it in bright colours, screw in some hooks and use it to keep an attractive garden record of what you have planted.

■ ABOVE
A row of pea sticks has a special appeal, because the twiggy branches refuse to be regimented in the vegetable garden, and have the appearance of a wild hedgerow up which the peas are scrambling. However, they are extremely practical, as the tangled twigs offer plenty of support.

■ ABOVE
Soldier-like bamboo canes take on an even more regimental appearance when the plants have their labels tied uniformly along the line.

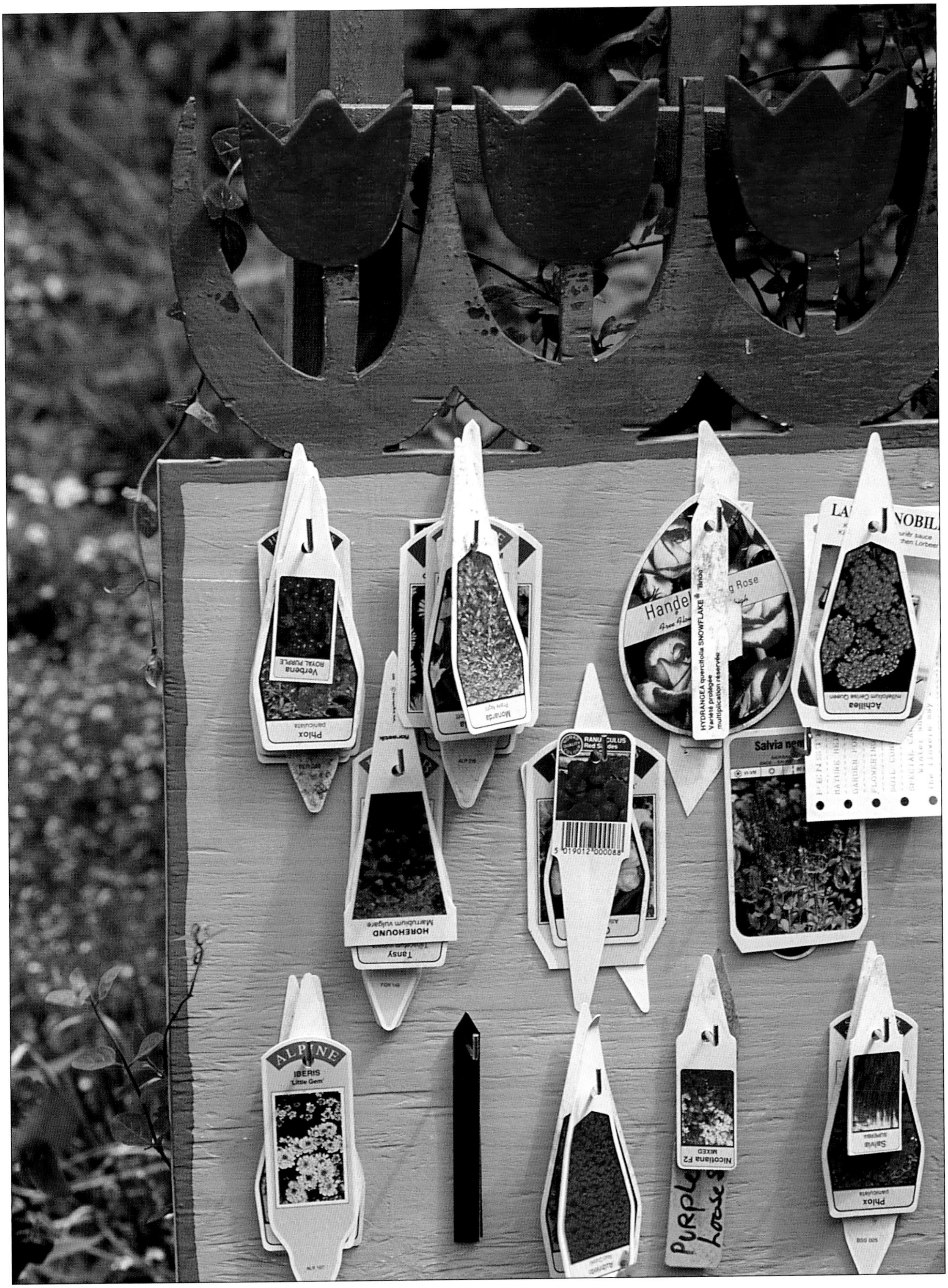
Verbena
ROYAL PURPLE
Phlox
paniculata
Monarda
HOREHOUND
Marrubium vulgare
Tansy
HYDRANGEA quercifolia SNOWFLAKE® 'Brido'
Variété protégée
multiplication réservée
Achillea
RANUNCULUS
Red Shades
ALPINE
IBERIS
'Little Gem'
Nicotiana F2
MIXED
Salvia
superba
Phlox
paniculata

Chicken Box Plant Stand

It is fun, especially in spring when the plants are low, to hoist a few flowers on high. And here is a witty way to achieve that: make a decorative wooden chicken nesting on a box, raise it on a stake and fill the box with pots of seasonal flowers.

■ OPPOSITE
Use this bright wooden chicken to bring a splash of instant colour to any part of the garden that needs perking up for a week or two as the seasons change.

1 Draw the chicken shape on paper, with a box back for it to stand on measuring 17 x 9cm/6½ x 3½in. Cut out the template and transfer the design to the MDF. Cut out using a jigsaw. Cut three pieces of plywood 17 x 9cm/6½ x 3½in and one piece 17 x 5cm/6½ x 2in.

2 Screw the two larger plywood panels to the chicken, one on either side. Screw the narrower panel between them, 3cm/1in from the bottom edge of the side panels, to make the base. Screw the final plywood panel onto the front.

Tools and Materials

- pencil
- paper
- tape measure
- scissors
- MDF (medium density fiberboard), 60 x 60cm/2 x 2ft
- jigsaw
- 25mm/1in plywood, at least 75 x 45cm/30 x 18in
- 6 screws
- screwdriver
- undercoat
- paintbrushes
- enamel paint in red, orange, white, blue, black and green
- 7.5 x 5cm/3 x 2in post, about 120cm/4ft long

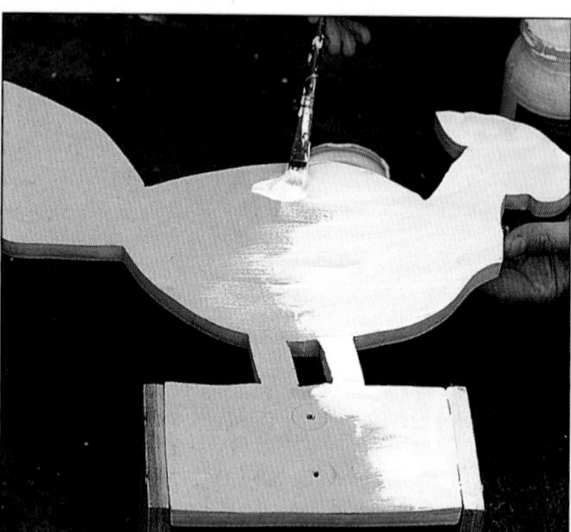

3 Paint both sides of the chicken and the box with a layer of undercoat and allow to dry.

4 Sketch the chicken's features on both sides of the chicken shape and paint with enamel paints. Paint the box green. Allow to dry overnight.

5 Screw the post to the back of the box to allow it to stand upright.

Wind Chimes

A walk on the beach or in the woods to gather weathered driftwood and twigs, and a forage in the potting shed, will provide you with all the materials you need to make these rustic wind chimes. The bells are made from miniature terracotta pots with metal vine-eyes as clappers. Provided the pots have no cracks, the wind chimes will sound like distant cow-bells, adding the extra dimension of gentle sounds to the sensual delights of your garden.

Tools and Materials

- wire cutters
- galvanized wire
- drill and bit
- 3 corks
- 4 weathered twigs of different sizes, the largest 30cm/12in long
- 2 metal vine-eyes
- 2 miniature terracotta pots

1 Cut one 50cm/20in and two 30cm/12in lengths of wire. Drill a hole through the centre of each cork. Make a hanging loop at one end of the longer piece of wire. Just beneath the loop, twist the wire around the centre of the longest twig and thread on a cork.

2 Add the next twig, either twisting the wire around it as before, or drilling a hole and threading it on. Add a second cork, followed by the third twig and the third cork. Make a hook in the end of the remaining wire, trimming it if necessary. Drill a hole through one end of the final twig and hook it on to the wire.

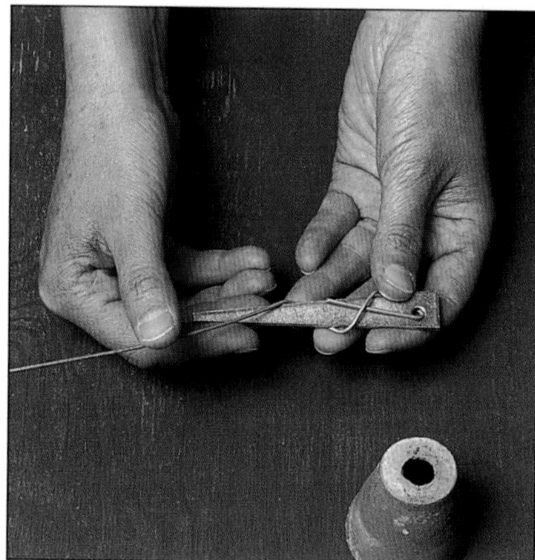

3 Thread a vine-eye on to each of the shorter lengths of wire and bend over 2.5cm/1in of the wire so that it lies flat against the vine-eye. Wrap the long end of the wire around the vine-eye in a spiral. Thread each vine-eye through the drainage hole in one of the terracotta pots, so that the wide end of the vine-eye becomes the clapper and the narrow end protrudes from the pot

4 Hang up the wind chimes and attach the bells, making sure that the wind chimes balance. Twist the wires protruding from the bells securely around the twig.

■ OPPOSITE
Wind chimes made with natural materials found in the garden blend effortlessly into its decorative scheme.

■ RIGHT
The charm of this alternative wind chime lies in its simplicity. Sand dollars provide the form, while the cockle shells strung onto raffia provide the music.

Seaworn Shell Mobile

Spend a day on the beach hunting among the rocks and pebbles and you are bound to come across plenty of materials for this delicate mobile. Limpet shells worn by the sea and sand often develop central holes, which makes them perfect for stringing. The stone-effect beads used here come in a range of smooth shapes and natural colours. Real pebbles that have weathered holes in them could also be used, but they might be too heavy to allow the mobile to move in the breeze.

1 Drill a hole through both ends of two pieces of driftwood, each about 36cm/14in long. Cut two 56cm/22in lengths of string and knot a bead 3cm/1in from the end of each. Thread one end of each piece of string through the hole in the driftwood for the top of the frame, and secure with a knot. Thread the other end through the hole in the bottom piece of wood. Thread a small, drilled cockle shell on to the end of each piece of string and secure with a knot.

2 To make the limpet wind chime, drill six holes, about 2cm/¾in apart, along a small piece of driftwood. Cut six 38cm/15in lengths of rough string. Thread and tie the limpet shells on to the strings and thread through the holes in the driftwood. Secure with knots and cut off any excess string.

Tools and Materials

- assorted pieces of driftwood
- drill
- scissors
- rough string
- assorted stone-effect beads
- 2 cockle shells
- weathered limpet shells
- natural raffia
- large winkle (periwinkle) shell
- 5 conch shells
- epoxy resin glue
- sticky tape

3 For the tailed winkle (periwinkle) shell, cut some short lengths of raffia and glue four or five into the mouth of each conch shell, using epoxy resin glue. Leave to dry. Drill a hole in the top of the large winkle shell.

4 Make a plait with three long strands of raffia, bind one end with tape and thread it through the hole in the winkle shell. Tie a knot in the end of the plait and pull it inside the shell. Tie beads and small pieces of driftwood on to the plait.

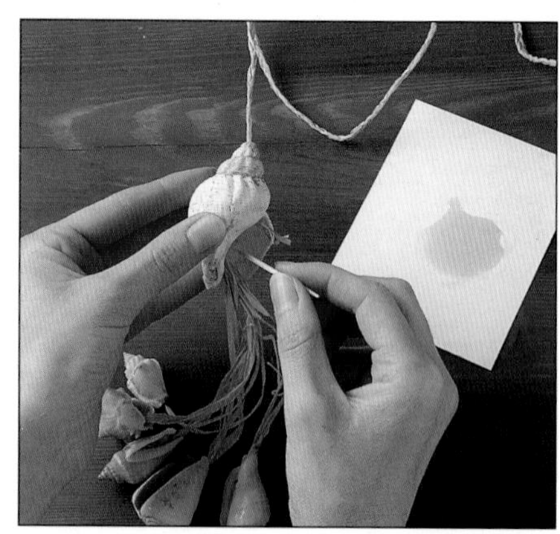

5 Gather together the conch shells and glue the ends of their raffia tails inside the mouth of the winkle shell, so that the shells hang down like a tail.

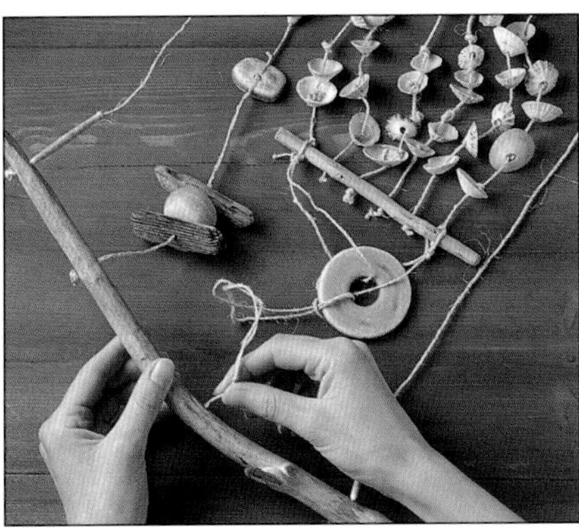

6 To assemble the mobile, drill two holes in the top of the frame. Thread the raffia plait through one of the holes and knot at the top. Tie a doubled length of string to each end of the top of the wind chime. Tie both strings around a large, round bead, then thread the ends through the second hole in the top of the frame and secure with a knot.

■ ABOVE
Hang the shell mobile where it will catch the breeze and its gentle tinkling will remind you of days at the seaside.

MOSAIC HEARTS

Most gardens are a source of treasure, however modest it might be. As you turn the soil, you are almost bound to uncover broken and weathered pieces of china and glass: save them to make decorative small mosaics. There is a real sense of satisfaction to be gained from turning a previous gardener's discarded rubbish into something attractive.

■ OPPOSITE
Pieces of weathered green glass set in tile cement are used to make these pretty hearts, moulded in biscuit (cookie) cutters. Hang the hearts on a wall or fence, or you could set them within a rock garden.

1 Use your fingers to coat the inside of the biscuit (cookie) cutter with a layer of petroleum jelly so that removing the finished mosaic heart will be easier. Wear rubber gloves if you prefer.

2 Cut a short length of garden wire and bend it into a loop. Position the loop at the top of the heart with the end of the wire under the edge of the mould and bent up inside it.

TOOLS AND MATERIALS

- heart-shaped biscuit (cookie) cutter
- petroleum jelly
- rubber gloves (optional)
- green garden wire
- scissors
- thick cardboard
- ready-mixed tile cement
- weathered pieces of glass

3 Place the mould on the sheet of cardboard to protect your work surface, and half fill it with the tile cement. Smooth the surface of the cement, using your fingers.

4 Press the pieces of glass on to the surface of the cement. Leave the mosaic to dry for at least 24 hours.

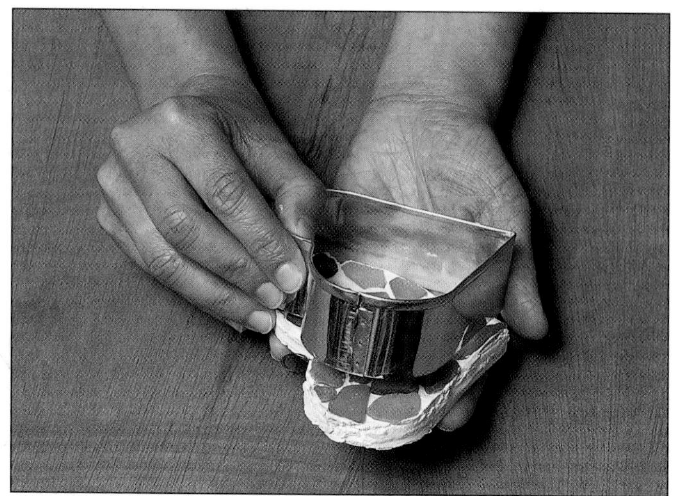

5 When the cement feels solid to the touch, gently remove the mosaic from the mould. Leave the mosaic to dry completely before taking it outside.

HEARTS IN THE GARDEN

Hearts hold universal appeal, and there is no reason why they shouldn't find a home in the garden. You will be surprised by what you can make from the most rudimentary weather-proof materials. Garden wire, chicken wire, twigs and raffia are all ideal. The beauty of the heart shape is that it is very easy to achieve. Just start with a circle of wire and bend it into a dip at one side and a point at the other. Twigs can be coaxed into curves to make the two halves of a heart, then bound together at the top and bottom.

■ ABOVE
A simple chicken wire heart decorated and suspended with paper string makes a pretty decoration for a shed door or the bare side of a wall in a sheltered spot.

■ ABOVE
This heart-shaped wreath carries a seasonal message. The twig framework is wound with variegated ivy and red berries, with a Christmas rose to finish.

■ ABOVE
A heart made from garden wire is knotted all around with sturdy bundles of natural raffia dyed green and ochre.

■ LEFT
Few things can be more romantic than a lavender heart. Make this with fresh lavender bound on to a wire frame, then let it dry naturally.

WIRE HEART

This delightful filigree heart is not difficult to make from ordinary garden wire, and it is certainly robust enough to withstand a winter outside. It is composed of small hearts bent into shape with pliers, then wired together in a beautiful overall design. Make one to hang in a tree, or make several in different sizes, so that they take on a sculptural quality. This one, flanked on all sides by neatly trimmed trees, is given throne-like importance.

TOOLS AND MATERIALS

- wire cutters
- medium-gauge garden wire
- pliers
- florist's or fuse wire
- raffia for hanging

1 Make several small heart shapes in various sizes by cutting short pieces of wire, bending them in half and curling the ends with pliers.

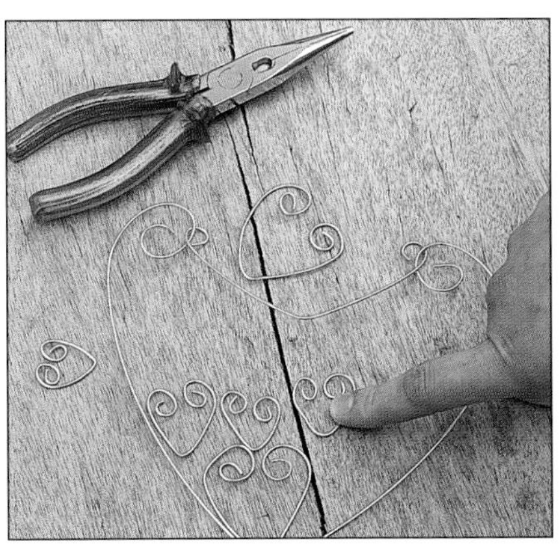

2 To make the large heart shape, cut a length of wire, bend it in half for the bottom of the heart and make a loop in each end. Cut a shorter length and form a loop at each end for the top. Link the looped ends to complete the outline. Lay the small hearts inside the frame as you make them, until they fill the shape.

■ BELOW
This fanciful little heart makes an unexpected garden detail – all the prettier because it is a surprise that so delicate a decoration should be made with ordinary garden wire.

3 Using florist's or fuse wire, bind the small hearts to the large heart and to each other where they touch, until the whole ensemble is stable. Make a hanger from raffia.

House Number Plaque

A mosaic number plaque will add a distinctive touch to your front entrance, hanging beside the door frame, or fixed to the garden gate. The tesserae for this design are cut from brightly coloured ceramic tiles, with fragments of mirror to enliven the background. As this mosaic is going to have to face all weathers, it's a good idea to paint the grouted areas with a transparent water sealant, but if you do this, clean any sealant from the surface of the tiles before it dries.

Tools and Materials

- 1cm/½in chipboard
- jigsaw
- pencil
- tape measure
- marker pen
- PVA (white) glue
- paintbrushes
- tile nippers
- selection of old china
- mirror fragments
- waterproof tile adhesive
- flexible (putty) knife
- damp cloth
- black weatherproof tile grout
- sponge
- exterior paint
- clip, for hanging
- soft cloth
- clear glass cleaner

1 Cut a piece of chipboard to size for the plaque. Draw the house number on the board, making each stroke at least 1.5cm/⅝in wide. Mark the positions for the mirror pieces.

2 Paint the chipboard all over, including the edges, with a coat of diluted PVA (white) glue. Leave to dry thoroughly.

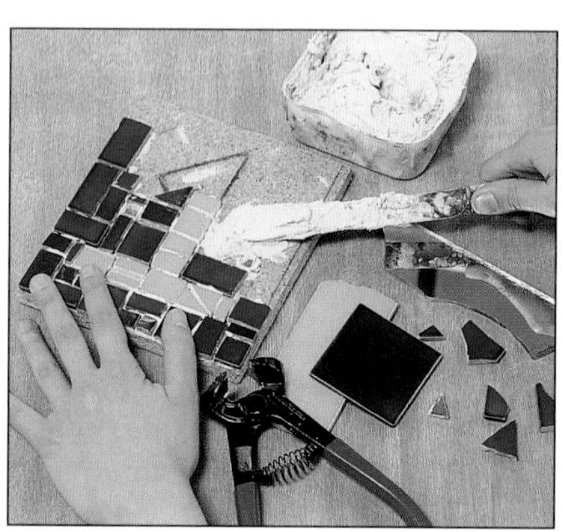

3 Cut the china and mirror into small pieces using tile nippers. Tile the number first, sticking on the pieces using waterproof tile adhesive. Fill in the background, cutting and applying small pieces of mirror, randomly spaced. Wipe off any excess adhesive with a damp cloth and leave the plaque to dry for 24 hours.

4 Cover the surface with black weatherproof tile grout, making sure all the gaps are filled. Spread the grout along the edges of the plaque, and let dry for 10 minutes. Wipe off excess grout with a sponge and leave to dry for 24 hours. Paint the back of the plaque with exterior paint and fix a clip for hanging. Polish the surface of the mosaic with a soft cloth and clear glass cleaner.

■ OPPOSITE
Mosaic is hard-wearing and weatherproof. Use strongly contrasting colours for the number so that it can be read from a distance.

Enjoying Your Garden Room

To get the most pleasure from your garden, you need to make it a comfortable space to live in. The place where you want to spend your leisure time should be somewhere that combines all the best aspects of your garden: it will be well secluded, yet will have plenty to look at, perhaps with fragrant plants and a water feature.

Once you have created the perfect spot you will want to share it with others from time to time. Outdoor parties can be great fun, whether the event is a simple lunch, a birthday tea or a romantic dinner for two. Lighting will help to create atmosphere, and offers lots of choices, from magical fairy lights to scented oil lamps or insect-repellent candles.

Theme your party table by decking it out in dusky ocean blues or vivid Mediterranean colours. As a final flourish, make an arrangement of sweet-smelling flowers or decorative garden produce for that just-right table centrepiece.

■ ABOVE
Once you have decorated your outdoor space, it's just a question of lighting the lamps and living in it. Warm summer evenings have never been so enjoyable.

■ OPPOSITE
The charm of a beautifully thought-out garden room is hard to resist.

Creating a Comfortable Space

If you set up a comfortable living area in the garden, you are much more likely to use it. With table and chairs standing ready, it is so much easier to bring the coffee and rolls out for breakfast al fresco. When an area is set aside for the children to play in, they will much more readily spend time outside. The priority is to earmark a sheltered living area with a cosy, room-like feel. If it is not next to the house, it will need to be screened by hedges or trellis to lend a sense of intimacy. You don't need a large space – just think how cramped some restaurants can be, yet once seated you feel comfortable.

■ OPPOSITE
Instead of lighting the table with candles for dinner on summer evenings, you could use oil lamps instead, scenting the lamp oil with a few drops of lavender essential oil to create a romantic and aromatic atmosphere.

Once the living area is established, try to incorporate something that stimulates each of the senses. Place a handsome specimen plant within view of the seating area or position the chairs to look on to a pleasant vista. Nature will offer plenty to please your ear: summer birdsong, the hum of bees and the whisper of trees and shrubs gently stirred by a breeze can be enhanced by the music of wind chimes, and a water feature can offer the relaxing sound of trickling water.

For fragrance, site plants with richly perfumed blooms near the seating area. Old-fashioned roses and honeysuckle are hard to beat, or try aromatic lavender and rosemary. Many flowers exude most scent at night: summer jasmine and tobacco plants (nicotiana) are two favourites. For touch, you can plant a contrast of textures, from feathery love-in-a-mist and ferns to luxuriant succulents. Finally, taste can be stimulated by nearby aromatic herbs or fragrant fruits such as strawberries and blackberries.

■ ABOVE
Lunch taken outside in the summer can be a memorable occasion. Attractive garden furniture and a pretty wild flower arrangement create a restful ambience, while fresh fruits and salads look wonderful set out on colourful china.

■ ABOVE
Throw a blue-checked cloth over the garden table, add some seasonal potted plants, and you have the perfect setting for drinks outside on a sunny day, even in early spring.

Animal Friends

Even in the densest urban areas, the outdoors is not devoid of wildlife. Countless wild creatures consider our gardens to be their home. Many of them we very much welcome, and we delight in watching their activities. And wild creatures can often be very useful as they help to maintain the ecological balance, eating unwanted guests such as greenfly and other pests.

Most wild garden visitors like to be self-catering and will not hesitate to organize their own homes, though with a little encouragement, such as the provision of a shallow dish of fresh water, they will appreciatively settle on your plot. Some plants attract beneficial insects such as butterflies and bees. The most obvious ones are the more highly scented species such as buddleia (known for this reason as the butterfly bush), lavender and honeysuckle. Birds can be encouraged by birdtables in the winter and birdbaths in the summer. Toads, which are consummate devourers of flies, like to set up house in cool, damp places – in flower pots laid on their sides in a leafy, damp private place, perhaps, or under a pile of stones. Once in residence, they usually stay and will make themselves useful, gradually working their way through the insect population almost as fast as it grows.

■ ABOVE
Butterflies can be attracted into the garden by planting their favourite nectar-rich flowering plants, such as buddleia and this exquisite pink autumn-flowering sedum.

■ LEFT
A birdbath is not only essential for garden birds, but can also become a piece of sculpture. This mosaic bowl nestles in a bed of marigolds and wallflowers.

■ ABOVE
A simply-made bird-feeding table will help encourage birds to visit.

■ RIGHT
Stir nuts and seeds into lard and mould the mixture into balls on lengths of string to provide a winter treat for the birds in your garden.

■ BELOW
String a selection of nuts on to a length of twine and hang it in an area of the garden, where you will be able to watch who is feeding and when.

LIGHTING EFFECTS

Enjoying the garden after nightfall is dependent on garden lighting, and in most domestic gardens, that is sadly lacking. If you are having your garden landscaped, you might like to consider having electricity cables laid and bringing in an expert to work out a plan. This would usually include general lighting, plus perhaps some spotlighting for focal points such as a favourite piece of statuary. But even if you don't want to go to that expense, there is a lot you can do.

■ OPPOSITE
Garden lighting adds its own special atmosphere – whether the event is an elaborate outdoor party or an evening of quiet seclusion.

Outdoor lighting will not achieve the same level of illumination as indoors, although this is rarely a problem: part of the appeal of being outside at night is the moody, shadowy lighting and being able to appreciate the moon and stars.

The easiest solution for general outdoor lighting is to fix a powerful halogen light to the outside of the house. Since the living areas of the garden are usually near the house, this should be ample. Another easy idea is to have an electrician fit an all-weather socket to the outside of the house. It is always useful to have access to electricity outdoors, but particularly if you wish to plug in both light and sound for fabulous evening entertainment. For special occasions you may like to hire all-weather strings of lights to hang in the trees. Plain white bulbs are particularly effective.

As well as the practical effects, such as showing changes of level or the edges of path, lighting also allows the best features of the garden to be highlighted while leaving others hidden, and brings the garden to life in a different and very special way.

■ ABOVE
This well-placed spotlight illuminates the textured edging of the stone urn, and makes a beautiful nightime display of the white petunias and lavandula 'Hidcote Pink'.

■ ABOVE
A lantern can be suspended from the same bracket as a hanging basket, where its soft light will enhance the flowers magically after sunset.

Candle Power

Candles must surely be the most romantic outdoor lighting. The light they cast is natural and flattering, holding the same fascination as any flame in the darkness, evoking ancient campfires and casting a magic circle of protective light around the table. They are also very practical for use in the garden as, unlike electric light, they are completely portable.

The ordinary candles you use on the dining table can simply be taken outside, candelabra and all, for a candle-lit dinner. If the night is at all breezy, use lanterns or some other holders which will protect the flames from the elements. Choose lanterns that will take substantially sized candles, otherwise you will be forever jumping up and down to light replacements. Also, check that the metalwork is robust, as some imported aluminium lanterns simply collapse once a candle flame melts the solder holding them together.

As well as lanterns, you could try Victorian night-lights, tumbler-like glass containers that hang on wires, huge glass hanging lanterns and candles in garden pots or galvanized buckets which – once they burn down below the rim – are protected from the wind. Candles that are specially designed to cope with the elements are garden flares, which produce a huge flame and can burn for up to three hours. The light they emit is surprisingly bright, which makes them ideal for general lighting or for lighting pathways.

You need to bear in mind when using outdoor candles and flares that the wind does blow the flame, so it is always important to position them well away from any foliage or furniture.

■ ABOVE
Lanterns provide perfect candle-light for the garden, as they protect the flame from the wind.

■ ABOVE
Garden flares produce a considerable amount of light. Many are also scented to help discourage insects.

■ RIGHT
Victorian night-lights hung on wires create a romantic glow in the trees.

■ ABOVE
This candle display cleverly emphasizes the beauty of garden paraphernalia: candles in vegetable shapes share the shelves with terracotta pots.

■ ABOVE
Adding candles needn't make for a fussy display. This simple supper table is casually dotted with groups of candles in soft pastel shades, complementing the colours of both the tableware and the potted plants, and pulling the different elements together to make a very natural-looking arrangement.

■ RIGHT
A large glass hanging lantern makes enchanting lighting for a special evening in the garden. Lotus-like flower candles float in water above a bed of shells in the glass lantern, looking like an exotic lily pond. Burning scented candles or fragranced essential oils would add to the effect.

Gilded Pots

Ordinary terracotta pots, gilded and filled with candle wax, make beautiful, sparkling garden lights. Use pots in a range of sizes and group them on tables, patios, walls and outdoor shelves for a magical effect in the soft evening light.

■ OPPOSITE
Fabulous golden pots glitter in the candle flames for a simple supper or an evening party in the garden.

Tools and Materials

- assorted terracotta pots
- self-hardening clay
- red oxide primer
- paintbrushes
- water-based gold size
- Dutch metal leaf in gold
- soft cloth or soft-bristled brush
- amber shellac
- artist's acrylic paint in white and aqua
- scissors
- wick
- wooden skewers
- candle wax
- double boiler

1 Plug the drainage hole of each pot with a little clay and leave to set. Prime the pots with red oxide primer and leave for 3–4 hours to dry

2 Apply a coat of water-based gold size and allow to dry for about 30 minutes, or until the size is transparent and tacky.

3 To apply the Dutch metal leaf, lift the sheets carefully and lay them on the size, gently smoothing each one with a cloth or soft-bristled brush. Brush off any excess leaf and polish gently with a soft cloth.

4 Apply a coat of amber shellac to seal the metal leaf and leave for at least 30 minutes until completely dry.

5 To age the pots, tint a little white acrylic with aqua and thin with water. Brush on the paint and rub off with a cloth. Leave to dry. Suspend a length of wick in each pot by tying it to a skewer laid across the top and check that it reaches the bottom. Melt the wax in a double boiler and pour it into the pot. Leave to set overnight.

CITRONELLA CANDLES

The pleasure of a summer evening in the garden, sitting around the table for a relaxing al fresco meal, can be quickly ruined by the presence of biting insects intent on their own feast. Candles scented with essential oils that have insect-repellent properties will serve a dual purpose: providing soft light and seeing off the enemy. Citronella oil is most commonly used as an insect repellent and is agreed to be the most effective, but if you dislike the scent you could use lavender, peppermint or a mixture of geranium and eucalyptus instead. On evenings when insects are particularly troublesome, add a few drops of the oil to an oil burner near the table, to encourage the insects to leave before you sit down to eat; these candles will then continue to act as a deterrent.

TOOLS AND MATERIALS

- 2 7.5cm/3in terracotta pots
- self-hardening clay
- 175g/6oz paraffin wax
- 50g/2oz natural beeswax
- heatproof bowl
- saucepan of simmering water or double boiler
- wooden spoon
- scissors
- wick
- 2 wooden skewers
- citronella essential oil

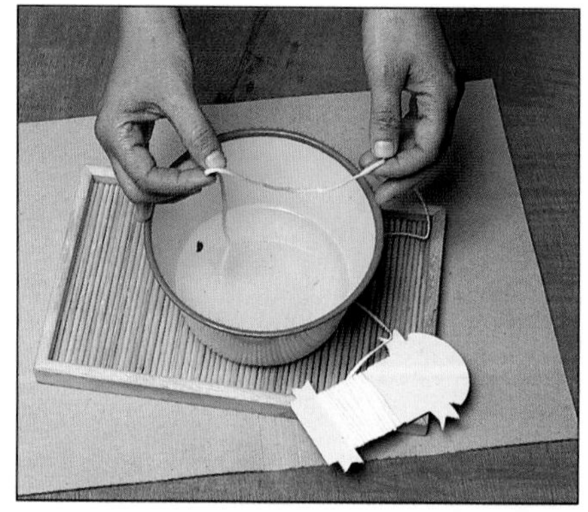

1 Plug the hole in the base of each of the terracotta pots with self-hardening clay and leave to set. Melt the paraffin wax and beeswax gently together in a heatproof bowl set over a saucepan of simmering water or in a double boiler over an electric ring or hotplate. Cut two 15cm/6in lengths of wick and dip into the wax. Leave for a several minutes to harden. Return the bowl frequently to the saucepan to prevent the wax from setting.

2 Rest the skewers across the pots. Position each wick to hang centrally in the pot and fold the end of the wick over the skewer. Add the essential oil to the wax and stir well to mix.

3 Pour the wax into the pots to just below the rim, tapping the sides of the pot to release any air bubbles. Reserve the remaining wax. As the candles cool, a dip will form around each wick. Remelt the wax and fill this dip with the remaining wax. Trim the wicks.

■ OPPOSITE
Candles in terracotta pots make pretty lights for evening parties outdoors, and these lemon-scented candles have the added benefit of keeping insects at bay.

IRON LANTERN

Give a new aluminium lantern the more appealing appearance of aged iron. Even the simplest shapes and brashest finishes become infinitely more pleasing when given the well-worn look of a lantern of yore.

TOOLS AND MATERIALS

- masking tape
- metal lantern
- medium-grade sandpaper
- white metal primer
- paintbrushes
- silver paint
- small natural sponge
- emulsion (latex) paint in black
- artist's acrylic paint in red oxide
- water spray
- satin polyurethane varnish
- varnish brush

1 Stick masking tape over all the glass of the lantern. Sand the metal to provide a key. Paint all the metal parts of the lantern with a coat of metal primer. Allow to dry for 2–3 hours, then paint on a silver base coat.

2 Dip the natural sponge into black emulsion (latex) and dab on to the lantern. Allow to dry for 1–2 hours.

3 Mix red oxide acrylic paint with a little water and, using an artist's paintbrush, drip this down the lantern to resemble rust. Spray with a water spray. Allow to dry for 1–2 hours. Varnish, leave to dry, then remove the tape.

■ BELOW
Subtle and darkly interesting, this lantern gains an antique quality once it has been painted.

Glass Jar Night-light

When lit with a small candle, this stained-glass night-light throws patches of coloured light on to the surrounding foliage. One jar is used as the base and another is broken into small fragments that are painted with glass paints. The fragments are then stuck on to the base jar and the gaps grouted. If your jars are not the same size, use the smaller one as the base.

Tools and Materials

2 glass jars
old dish towel
goggles
protective gloves
hammer
scrap paper
newspaper
reusable adhesive
glass paints
paintbrushes
solvent-free, rapid setting epoxy resin glue
white cellulose filler
grout spreader
scourer
sandpaper
acrylic paint

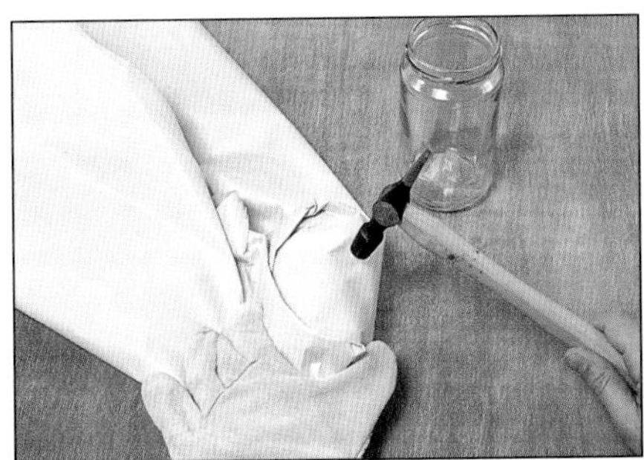

1 Wrap a jar in a dish towel. Wearing goggles and gloves, and covering your hair, smash the jar with a hammer. Place the pieces to be used as tesserae on scrap paper with the sharp edges facing downwards to avoid cutting yourself. Wrap the unused glass in newspaper and dispose of it carefully.

2 Use reusable adhesive to pick up the broken pieces of glass and turn them over so that the sharp edges face upwards. Paint the concave surface of each fragment with glass paint in different colours. Leave to dry. Glue the painted fragments to the base jar using solvent-free epoxy resin glue. Leave until completely dry.

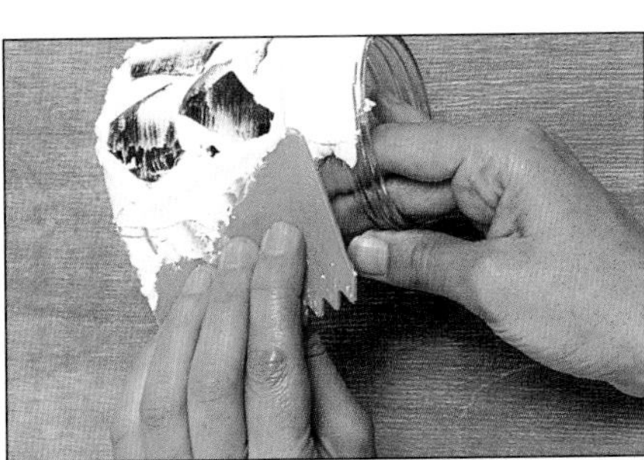

3 Spread cellulose filler over the surface, smoothing it into the top and bottom edges of the jar, and wiping off any excess. Let dry. If any cracks appear as it dries, smooth over more filler. When dry, clean off excess filler with a scourer and water, and sandpaper. Paint over the filler with acrylic paint.

■ RIGHT
This delightful lantern gives a subtle glow in the garden at night, looking like a miniature stained-glass window.

ENTERTAINING OUTSIDE

What a joy it is, when all is said and done, to invite friends over and relax together in the garden. It is the wonderful casualness of al fresco eating that is so appealing. The food can be simple: fresh salads, vegetables and fruits, perhaps home-grown. Meat or fish can be grilled or barbecued with fresh herbs, the aroma complementing the scent of the herbs growing in the beds. Add some bread and a couple of bottles of wine and you have all the ingredients necessary for a memorable occasion.

■ RIGHT
Use your own fresh garden herbs in pretty and delicious summer drinks when entertaining in the garden. Freeze snippets of herbs and edible flowers into ice cubes as a finishing touch.

Decorating the outdoor table is wonderfully effortless. All you need for a stunning evening party is a table centrepiece of fresh seasonal flowers or potted plants from the garden, and a collection of candles to softly light the scene.

■ RIGHT
Teatime, when the heat of the day is subsiding, is a wonderful time to get together in the garden, even if it's just for a cup of tea and a chat.

■ BELOW
With the gentle sounds of the garden and the heady perfume of flowers in the hot afternoon sun, an informal gathering will become a memorable occasion.

DECORATING TABLES WITH A THEME

Out in the garden as well as indoors, a thoughtfully decorated table will charm your guests, stimulating conversation and appetite, and making your dinner party a visual as well as an edible feast. Let your surroundings dictate the styling of your table: in place of crisp white damask and silver, let the colour and naturalness of the garden setting spill on to the table, with simple pots of flowers picked from the borders, organic materials like wood, raffia and shells, and rustic dishes in earthy browns and creams, or bright sunny glazes.

■ ABOVE
Blue and white are classic colours for china, reminiscent of old Chinese designs and traditional English patterns. Blues on blues make a wonderful mix, looking especially beautiful under the blue sky of a summer's day. You can keep to lavender blues, lean towards greener denim blues or mix them all together: blend at least three shades to achieve a pleasing overall effect. White and blue look fresh and clean together, and this combination is readily available in both table linen and china. Dried lavender is the ideal material for an everlasting table decoration in this setting, or make a simple arrangement of newly-picked fresh flowers in white.

■ ABOVE

The neutral tones and beguiling forms found on the beach provide wonderful inspiration for table decorations. The silvery greys and soft beiges of pebbles, driftwood and old galvanized metal, teamed with the coral pinks of shells and sea-washed terracotta, create a winning combination. Simplicity is the key: a bowl of mussel shells set beside a jar of wild flowers are enough to suggest the subtle tones of a seashore table setting. Even a naturally-sculptured piece of driftwood by itself would make a wonderfully elegant centrepiece.

■ BELOW

Evoking hot summer days in Greece, Portugal or Provence, this sun-filled Mediterranean style is simple, rustic and colourful. The typical palette is chalky blue and turquoise set against sun-baked terracotta and white. Paint is a favourite medium in the Mediterranean, and everything is given a lick of colour: woodwork, furniture, tableware; even old cans can be turned into decorative containers. Here, old plates and bowls have been painted and decorated with simple but striking designs and napkins boldly embroidered. Vibrantly coloured flowers add the finishing touch before the guests are seated, the wine starts to flow and the hors d'oevres arrive.

■ RIGHT
Much of the joy of entertaining outdoors is the impromptu feel of the occasion: you can make a beautiful table by simply gathering together whatever is in season and allowing that to govern your colour scheme. Marigolds, iris leaves and tree ivy were the starting point for this elaborate setting.

■ RIGHT
Arranging a table on a theme is very easily achieved: decide the theme, then gather together crockery and table linen which will tie in with your chosen style. The synchronization of colours alone can be enough to suggest a harmonious arrangement.

TABLE DECORATIONS

Outdoor table centres are the very easiest to put together because they are at their most successful when they complement their surroundings. So plunder the garden and then combine the ingredients with flair. You may cut a few flowers, add foliage or even fruit and vegetables; or you may simply gather together some of the smaller plants in pots from around the garden. The concentration on a table of what grows in naturally looser arrangements throughout the garden serves to focus the overall look.

■ ABOVE
Ivy plants in sundae-glass shaped galvanized containers, accessorized with a couple of canes pastel-painted to look like straws, make a witty cocktail table centrepiece.

■ LEFT
In summer, potted strawberry plants are easily transformed when they are held in a wire container and accessorized with a few ripe fruits.

■ RIGHT
In a wire basket woven with natural raffia, pots of verbena are gathered together and surrounded with tiny pots of variegated ivy. The resulting arrangement is casually beautiful, perfectly in accord with its setting.

■ BELOW
Ornamental cabbages make an unusual table centrepiece, very appropriate to the garden table. The cabbages are complemented by individual leaves decorating the napkins.

■ LEFT
The sun-drenched colours of the Mediterranean pervade this vibrant dried flower arrangement in a raffia-tied terracotta pot, perfectly partnered by a vivid Provençal cotton tablecloth.

■ ABOVE
Decorate the table with a romantic herbal dish, which you can fill with strawberries or other soft fruits. Simply set a bowl in the centre of a florist's foam ring lavishly filled with flowers and herbs. Enchanting daisy-like chamomile flowers have been set in an aromatic base of rosemary and oregano to make an arrangement reminiscent of a summer meadow.

■ LEFT
The ruffled charm of this sage arrangement makes a deliciously aromatic, softly coloured table centre, co-ordinated with rosemary napkin ties.

■ RIGHT
Wild-looking flowers make the prettiest table garlands for summer celebration meals. Garlands do use a lot of material, so if you don't have enough suitable flowers in the garden, look in the florist's for cultivated versions of those that grow wild. This garland is a combination of frothy white dill, green bupleurum and purple knapweed.

■ ABOVE
This herbal ring of mint, flat-leaf parsley and fennel flowers makes a sophisticated green frame for summer fruit, but if you prefer something a little more showy you could add some daisy flowers, such as feverfew, which would look charming.

■ RIGHT
This simple herbal tussie mussie is made from chive flowers, rosemary and comfrey, but the idea could be adapted so that any seasonal flowers can be used. The sweet-smelling herbs will scent the table throughout the meal.

Stay-put Tablecloth

Tablecloths on the garden table look pretty and fresh, but can quickly act like a sail if the slightest breeze starts up. Lunch ceases to be fun when the corner of the cloth is whipped up on to the table, dropping into the beetroot salad or knocking over a couple of glasses of wine. A weighted cloth is the solution to this inevitable problem of outdoor eating. Just slip some circular metal curtain weights into the corners of the cloth: they will keep it firmly in place, and can be quickly removed before laundering the tablecloth.

Tools and Materials

2m/2yds fabric, 1.5m/1½yds wide

scissors

iron

tape measure

sewing machine

matching sewing thread

15cm/6in heavy-duty self-adhesive Velcro

4 circular metal curtain weights

satin polyurethane varnish

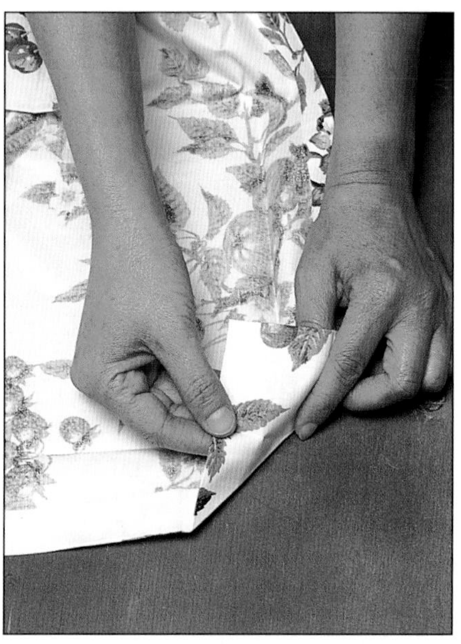

1 Fold the fabric diagonally across itself to make a right-angled triangle. Cut across the width, along the edge of the triangle, to make a square. (Make napkins from any extra fabric.)

2 Open out the fabric and fold in and press a 2.5cm/1in hem along all four edges. Fold in the corners of the cloth to make triangles 8cm/3¼in high, and press in place.

3 Fold over a 6cm/2½in around all edges and press to form a mitre at each corner. Stitch all around the cloth 5mm/¼in from the edge and again 5mm/¼in inside the edge of the hem.

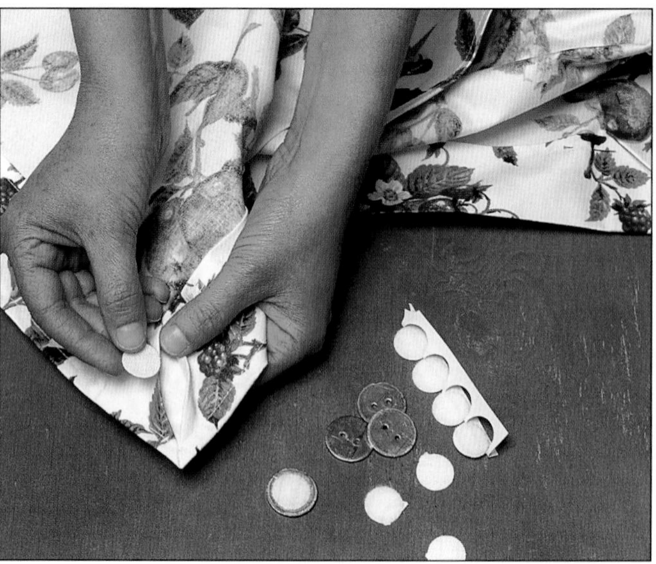

4 Remove the backing paper from a piece of Velcro, insert into one of the corner folds and stick in place. Attach the opposite piece of Velcro to one of the curtain weights. Repeat in the other three corners. When you are using the cloth, slip the weights into position and the Velcro will hold them in place.

■ **OPPOSITE** A weighted tablecloth can make all the difference to the success of a meal eaten outdoors.

Organdie Cloth

The lightness of exquisitely detailed guinea fowl feathers perfectly complements the delicate fabric of this tablecloth and, tucked into little tulle pockets, they are easy to remove for washing. Buy plenty of feathers as you need to be able to select at least 24 of a similar size. Bunches of extra feathers, secured by organdie ties, make charming details at the corners.

■ RIGHT
Delightful spotted guinea fowl feathers lend natural detail to a delicate organdie tablecloth, which would be perfect to set on the table for afternoon tea.

Tools and Materials

- 110 x 120cm/43in x 4ft white cotton organdie
- scissors
- needle
- white sewing thread
- 100 x 10cm/39 x 4in white tulle
- pins
- white stranded embroidery thread
- 24 guinea fowl feathers

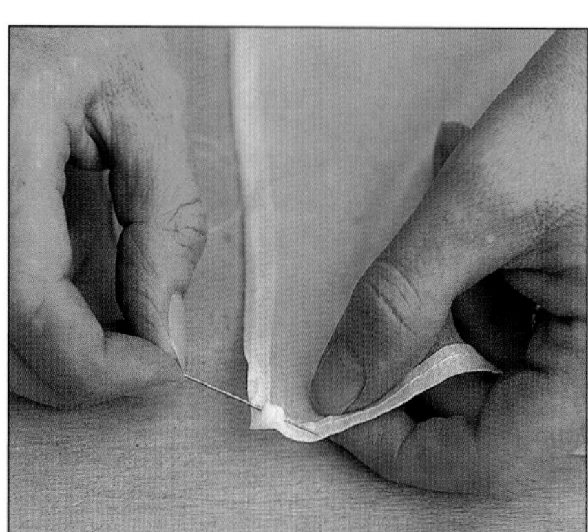

1 Trim the organdie to make a 110cm/43in square. Turn in and stitch a double hem around all four sides. Cut the tulle into 12 rectangles about 7.5 x 5cm/3 x 2in.

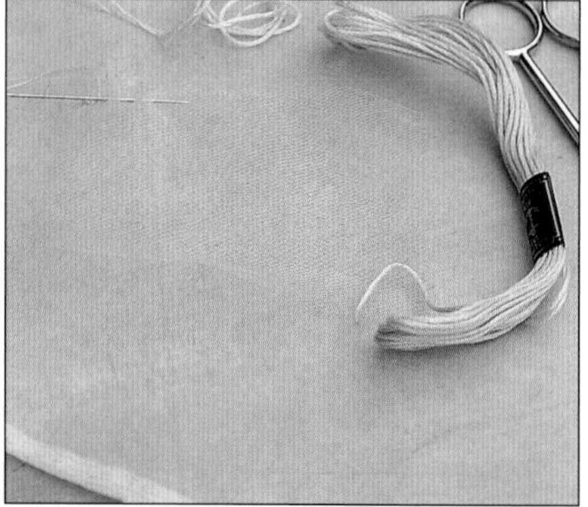

2 Pin the pockets on to the cloth: arrange four in a diagonal line from corner to corner, and a parallel row of three on either side, and one near the remaining corners. Stitch each pocket around three sides, leaving one short side open.

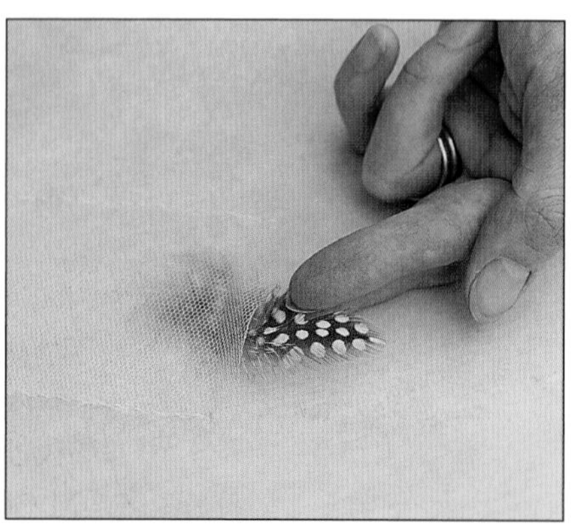

3 Select 12 similar-sized guinea fowl feathers, and slip one into each pocket, quill end first. For each corner of the tablecloth, cut a strip of organdie about 22 x 2.5cm/8¾ x 1in.

4 Fold the organdie strips in half lengthways, turn in the sides and ends and slipstitch all around to make a tie. Make a bunch of three feathers and stitch them to the middle of the tie. Tie the organdie in a knot around the feathers. Stitch (or tie, if you want to remove the feathers for washing) each feather trim to the tablecloth corners.

Cushions

You have arranged your favourite garden chair in the perfect place, or slung your hammock between two trees. You have a good book, a convenient table for your coffee and sunglasses. There is just one thing missing from this garden idyll: a blissful abundance of cushions, for your head, your back and your feet, so that you can drift away in perfect relaxation.

You could, of course, just pick up a cushion from inside the house and take it with you whenever you sit out, but it really is much nicer to have a separate collection of cushions for outdoor use only.

Even with the best intentions in the world, whatever you take outside will make contact with grass cuttings and fallen leaves, and these will conspire to limit the relaxation you are looking for.

■ ABOVE
The luscious corded and cutwork embroidered cushions lining this hammock make it irresistibly alluring.

■ ABOVE
A small linen cushion with a filling of dried lavender exudes its fabulous fragrance when warmed by the sun.

■ LEFT
Rest a weary head on a relaxing mixture of chamomile and lavender. Sewn inside the stuffing of a gingham cushion, the dried herbs will calm you down at the end of a hectic day.

■ RIGHT
Hang small cushions filled with herbs over the back of a chair to bestow a delicious waft of scent when you sit down.

■ RIGHT
Hops are too pretty to hide, so if you want to take advantage of the relaxing qualities of their scent, use them to fill a cushion of fine muslin or gauze trimmed with lace rosettes.

Twiggy Tray

A tray of twigs is very easy to make and surprisingly robust – all for the cost of a few strands of raffia. This tray is made from young willow shoots, but any twigs will do as long as they're fairly straight and of a similar thickness. The end result is a tray that is wonderfully organic – perfect for outdoor apéritif drinks or a light lunch.

Tools and Materials

raffia
about 60 young willow (or similar) shoots, 45cm/18in long
secateurs (pruners)

1 For the base of the tray, fold one strand of raffia in half and place the end of one willow stick in the loop. Now bring the lower piece of raffia up and the upper piece down, enclosing the stick, and place the next stick between the two lengths of raffia.

2 Bring the lower piece up and the upper piece down again to enclose the next stick, and position the third stick. You will find that you soon develop a twisting rhythm. Continue until you have woven in 44 sticks. Weave in three more lines of raffia about 9cm/3½in apart down the length of the sticks and one near the other end, to create a firm, flat mat for the base.

3 Cut eight sticks to fit the short sides of the tray base. Make the first side of the tray by laying down four full-length sticks at right angles to four of the shorter sticks. Tie the middle of a strand of raffia around one of the long sticks. Place one of the short sticks at right angles on top of this and tie that in. Continue until all eight sticks are used up, then tie firmly to secure.

4 Create the other three corners in the same way until you have made up a rectangular frame that will become the sides of the tray.

5 Place the frame over the base. Feed the raffia into the side of the base at the end of one of the lines of weaving. As before, work the two ends of raffia up the side and down again, tying them together at the bottom. Repeat wherever the frame meets the ends of the woven raffia on the base, and at two equally spaced intervals along the short sides.

6 To attach the short sides, fold a piece of raffia in half and feed one end from underneath the base between two sticks, over the lowest frame stick and back between the sticks to meet the other end of the raffia. Tie underneath. Then bring one end up between the next two sticks, over the bottom frame stick, and down again. Tie the two ends together again tightly. Continue in this way until the width of the frame is tied to the base at one end. Repeat at the other end to complete the tray.

■ RIGHT
In an outdoor setting, an organic tray blends with the garden, and looks particularly charming.

■ ABOVE
Choose straight, even-sized young shoots for a neat result.

Decorative Gardener's Accessories

In the decorative garden, there's no reason why the tools and other accoutrements used by the gardener should not be just as beautiful to look at as everything else. Gardening is always a pleasure, but it can be enhanced even further if the equipment you use has its own visual appeal. Good, well-looked-after garden tools, with handles polished with use and age, have a beauty and integrity of their own. Decorative details will beautify the rest of your gardening paraphernalia too, so that you really enjoy every task in the garden.

■ ABOVE
Decorate a ready-made apron with flower pot pockets and brass rings, to hold all your gardening essentials.

■ ABOVE
If you have fruit to pick, make the job a real pleasure by gathering it in an elegant slatted basket. This one is stencilled with images of apples and pears and given an aged look with a coat of tinted varnish.

■ ABOVE
Find your boots easily among the pile at the back door by personalizing them with charming painted designs. Just use enamel paints and take your inspiration from the garden.

■ ABOVE
You could paint an alternative design on the other boot.

■ ABOVE
Hand tools with plain handles are easy to lose sight of in the summer border. Bright yellow paint and eye-catching insect stickers sealed with varnish make them hard to miss.

■ ABOVE
Small hand tools like trowels and forks are needed daily in the garden, so choose shapes that are comfortable to hold and a pleasure to use.

■ ABOVE
The traditional trug is a piece of garden equipment that has endured for many years and is still appreciated for its practicality, durability and fine design. Woodstains will not spoil its elegance, but they can give it individuality and provide a colour accent in the garden.

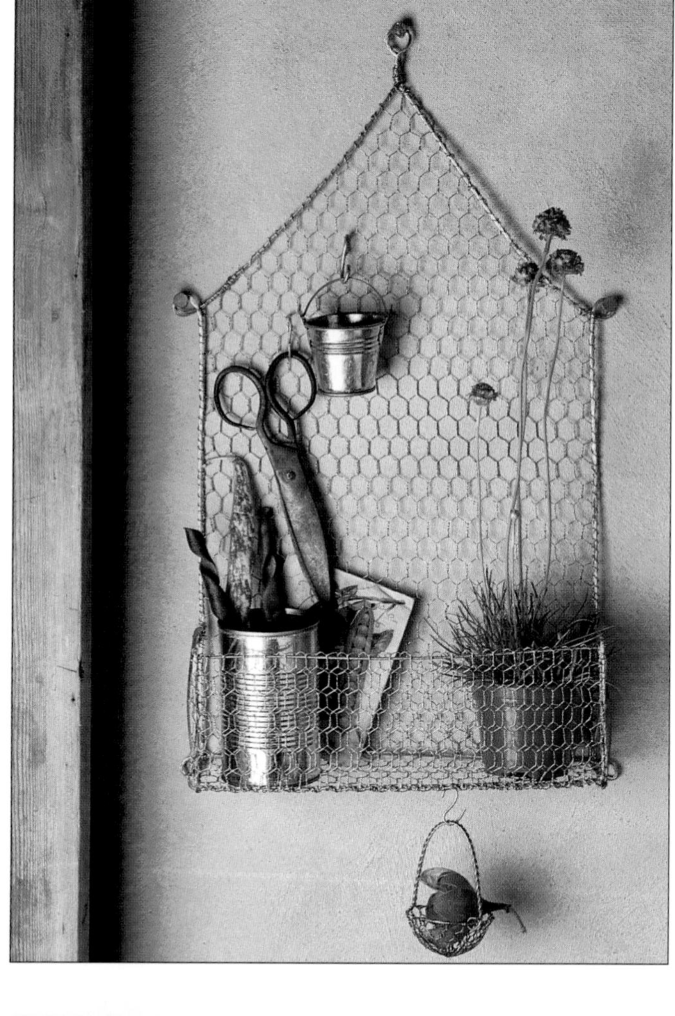

■ ABOVE
The potting shed tends to attract lots of bits and pieces, and this pretty rack will help to take care of them. Make a simple frame from lengths of garden wire and wrap a piece of chicken wire around it, binding it firmly to the frame with wire.

■ LEFT
Small storage drawers are handy for keeping fiddly accessories such as plant labels and rings. Label each drawer with an example of its contents so that you know exactly where they are.

■ ABOVE
Hessian bags are useful for storing bulbs that you have lifted after flowering, as they allow the bulbs to breathe. A picture of the contents, cut from the original bulb packaging, makes the bags look good in the potting shed.

■ ABOVE
If you collect your own seeds, store them prettily in home-made paper seed packets decorated with colour photocopies of your own photographs of the flowers. This is a lovely way to give surplus seed to fellow gardeners. Write details of the plant and instructions for cultivation on the back of the packet.

■ LEFT
A wooden box with a well-fitting lid is ideal for storing half-used packets of seeds that will still be viable next season. Decoupage, using old engravings of fruit and vegetables, makes an attractive and appropriate decoration for the lid.

INDEX

STOCKISTS AND SUPPLIERS

UNITED KINGDOM

Avant Garden
77 Ledbury Road
London W11 2AG
Tel: (0171) 229 4408
Wirework topiary frames, candle holders, wall sconces, candle baskets, terracotta pots

Brett Specialized Aggregates
Fordwich Road
Sturry
Kent CT2 0BW
Tel: (01227) 712876
Paving supplies

Clifton Little Venice
3 Warwick Place
London W9 2PS
Tel: (0171) 289 7894
Wirework and ironwork, topiary shapes, jardinieres and wall masks

Drummonds of Bramley
Horsham Road
Bramley
Guildford
Surrey GU5 0LA
Tel: (01483) 898766
Architectural salvage

Finnigans Hammerite
Hunting Specialised Products
Prudhoe
Northumberland NE42 6LP
Tel: (01661) 830000
Specialized single-coat metal paint, both spray-on and brush-on

Indian Ocean Trading Company
155–163 Balham Hill
London SW12
Tel: (0181) 675 4808
Wooden furniture and benches, deck-chairs, steamers and garden umbrellas

Keim Mineral Paints Ltd
Muckley Cross
Morville
Nr Bridgnorth
Shropshire WV16 4RR
Tel: (01746) 714543

Marshalls Mono
Southowram
Halifax HX3 9SY
Tel: (01422) 366666
Natural clay pavings and concrete block paving

Paint Magic Jocasta Innes
79 Shepperton Road
London N1 3DF
Tel: (0171) 354 9696
Decorative paint finishes that can be teamed with varnish for light outdoor use

Rusco Marketing
Little Faringdon Mill
Lechlade
Gloucester GL7 3QQ
Tel: (01367) 252 754
Wooden and metal garden furniture, umbrellas and hammocks

UNITED STATES

Exterior masonry paints, gloss paints, stains, varnishes, as well as concrete, granite and concrete stone pavings can be found in general hardware stores and home-improvement centres.

Alsto's Handy Helpers
P.O. Box 1267
Galesburg
IL 661401
Tel: (800) 447-0048
Cedar patio furniture and swings, metal lawn chairs, gliders

Ballard Designs
1670 DeFoor Avenue NW
Atlanta
GA 30318-7528
Tel: (404) 351-5099
Cast architectural ornaments, metal and glass chairs, benches and tables

Bamboo Fencer
31 Germania Street
Jamaica Plain
MA 02130
Tel: (800) 775-8641
Bamboo fencing

Bufftech
2525 Walden Avenue
Buffalo
NY 14225
Tel: (800) 333-0579
Vinyl fencing

Crescent Bronze Powder Co.
3400 N. Avondale Avenue
Chicago
IL 60618
Tel: (312) 529-2441
Metallic pigment paints and lacquer

Discount Pond Supplies
P.O. Box 423371H
Kissimmee
FL 34742-3371
Fax (407) 932-4019
Water garden supplies

Gardener's Eden
100 North Point Street
San Francisco
CA 94133
Tel: (800) 822-9600
Garden ornaments, metal, twig and wicker garden furniture

Hens & Feathers & Company
10 Balligomingo Road
Gulph Mills
PA 19428
Tel: (800) 282-1910
Urns, planters, fountains and statuary made from banded marble resin in hand-finished patinas

Materials Unlimited
2 West Michigan Avenue
Ypsilanti
MI 48197
Tel: (313) 483-6980
Cast iron fences, posts, gates

Woodcrafters
11840 N. U.S. 27
Dewitt
MI 48820
Woodcraft patterns, including windmills, wishing wells, weather vanes, bird houses, whirligigs and jigsaws

CANADA

Avant Gardener
2235 West 4th Avenue
Vancouver
BC V6K 1N9
Tel: (604) 736-0404

Creative Wood Products
88 Shoemaker Street
Unit 1
Kitchener
Ontario N2E G4
Quality cedar furniture

Cruikshanks Mail Order
Tel: 1-800-665-5605
Gardening supplies and accessories

Mason's Masonry Supply
6291 Netherhart Road
Mississauga
Ontario L5T 1A2
Paving supplies

AUSTRALIA

Amber Tiles
Tel: 132 241 for NSW stores
Tiles, slate, pavers, terracotta

Chris Cross
1575 Burke Road
Kew
Vic 3103
Tel: (03) 859 2666
Unusual landscape material

Cotswold Garden Furniture Pty Ltd
42 Hotham Parade
Artarmon
NSW 2064
Tel: (02) 9906 3686
Imported teak furniture

Elegant World Pty Ltd
73–75 Market Street
Condell Park
NSW 2200
Tel: (02) 708 5079
Pots, planters, fountains, birdbaths, statues, columns, balustrading, steps, paving, architectural monuments

The Lattice Factory
121 Church Street
Ryde
NSW 2112
Tel: (02) 809 7665
Pergolas, fences, planter boxes – all made to measure

Whitehouse Gardens
388 Springvale Road
Forest Hill
Vic 3131
Tel: (03) 877 1430
Statues, ponds, birdbaths, pots